BIBLE STUDY

DR. DAVID JEREMIAH

WHAT ARE YOU AFRAID OF?

FACING DOWN YOUR FEARS WITH FAITH

LifeWay Press®
Nashville, Tennessee

Published by LifeWay Press® • © 2013 David Jeremiah • Reprinted 2016

ISBN 978-1-4300-3180-2 • Item 005641764

Dewey decimal classification: 152.4
Subject headings: FEAR \ FAITH \ CHRISTIAN LIFE

To order additional copies of this resource, write to LifeWay Resources Customer Service; One LifeWay Plaza; Nashville, TN 37234-0113; fax 615.251.5933; phone toll free 800.458.2772; order online at *lifeway.com;* email *orderentry@lifeway.com;* or visit the LifeWay Christian Store serving you.

Printed in the United States of America

Groups Ministry Publishing • LifeWay Resources
One LifeWay Plaza • Nashville, TN 37234-0152

CONTENTS

THE AUTHOR

Dr. David Jeremiah serves as the senior pastor of Shadow Mountain Community Church in El Cajon, California. He is the founder and host of Turning Point, a ministry committed to providing Christians with sound Bible teaching relevant to today's changing times through radio and television, the Internet, live events, and resource materials and books. A best-selling author, Dr. Jeremiah has written more than 40 books, including *Captured by Grace, Living with Confidence in a Chaotic World, The Coming Economic Armageddon, God Loves You: He Always Has; He Always Will,* and *What in the World Is Going On?*

Dr. Jeremiah's commitment to teaching the complete Word of God makes him a sought-after speaker and writer. His passion for reaching the lost and encouraging believers in their faith is demonstrated through his faithful communication of biblical truths.

A dedicated family man, Dr. Jeremiah and his wife, Donna, have 4 grown children and 11 grandchildren.

INTRODUCTION

If you struggle with fear, you're not alone. Fear is no respecter of people. It strikes the weak and the powerful. It haunts the young and the old, the rich and the poor. Even those who seem to have it all, including celebrities and "fearless" leaders, have confessed to ongoing struggles with fear.

Take George Washington, for example. Although he served as one of America's founding fathers, he was scared to death of being buried alive. Richard Nixon was terrified of hospitals, and Napoleon Bonaparte—the military and political genius—was afraid of cats. Those examples are somewhat humorous, but in reality there's very little to find funny about fear and the way it affects our everyday lives.

To be frank, I didn't write this study to address the kinds of isolated phobias that affect tiny percentages of the population. Instead, I wrote this study because I see fear as a real and present danger in the body of Christ.

Many Christians are besieged and enslaved each day by a wide variety of fears, including the following.

- Defeat: the fear of failure
- Depression: the fear of mental breakdown
- Disconnection: the fear of being alone
- Disease: the fear of serious illness
- Death: the fear of dying
- Deity: the fear of God

Those are the most common fears I've encountered through my decades of ministry, both personally and in the lives of church members. I encourage you to examine those fears throughout this study in the weeks to come. I also encourage you to take a deeper look at these fears—and explore several others that aren't addressed here—by reading my book *What Are You Afraid Of?* (Tyndale, 2013; ISBN 978-1-4143-8046-9).

As you engage with these resources, I pray you'll grow in your conviction that God is the answer to all your fears. I pray when you look into the future, you'll see God's power and love guarding your every step. I pray you'll open your heart and mind to receive biblical truth that sets you free to live the fearless life God created you to enjoy.

DEFEAT: THE FEAR OF FAILURE

WELCOME TO THIS SMALL-GROUP DISCUSSION
OF WHAT ARE YOU AFRAID OF?

Because fear is a universal human experience, it's something everyone can relate to and talk about. To facilitate introductions and highlight the primary theme of this study, spend a few minutes answering the following questions about your experiences with fear. If possible, create the appropriate atmosphere by turning down the lights.

- What fears kept you up at night when you were a child?

- What fears have kept you awake at night in recent years?

- Describe the emotions and physical reactions that typically accompany your experiences with fear.

After everyone has had a chance to share, work as a group to identify the fears you've most commonly experienced, both as children and as adults.

This session will focus on defeat: the fear of failure. To prepare for the DVD segment, read aloud the following verses.

> *Fear the LORD, serve Him in sincerity and in truth, and put away the gods which your fathers served on the other side of the River and in Egypt. Serve the LORD! And if it seems evil to you to serve the LORD, choose for yourselves this day whom you will serve, whether the gods which your fathers served that were on the other side of the River, or the gods of the Amorites, in whose land you dwell. But as for me and my house, we will serve the LORD.*
> JOSHUA 24:14-15

WATCH

COMPLETE THE VIEWER GUIDE BELOW AS YOU WATCH DVD SESSION 1.

A person who is afflicted with the fear of failure considers the possibility of failing so intense that he chooses not even to take the _____.

OVERCOMING YOUR FEAR OF FAILURE

1. The principle of divine _____

2. The principle of divine _____

The more there is to _____ on, the less there is to fear about.
The less there is fear, the less there is _____.

3. The principle of divine _____

4. The principle of divine _____

Turn to the Word of God and find in it the strong words that will lift you up and set you _____ from your _____.

5. The principle of divine _____

6. The principle of divine _____

Whatever we're afraid of, whatever we're afraid to tackle, if _____ is with us, we don't have to be afraid.

God's commandments are God's _____.

RESPOND

What did you appreciate most in Dr. Jeremiah's teaching? Why?

How would you summarize the fear of failure and its effect on people's lives?

In what situations do you most often experience the fear of failure?

How do you typically encourage friends and family members who feel inadequate about themselves or their abilities?

When have you felt called by God to pursue a goal or engage in a task? How did you respond?

Dr. Jeremiah listed six principles through which God often helps us overcome the fear of failure: divine perspective, divine purpose, divine persuasion, divine priority, divine presence, and divine prosperity. What are your initial reactions to these principles?

What other factors have helped you overcome the fear of failure in the past?

APPLICATION. Intentionally take a risk this week that will force you to confront the fear of failure. This doesn't have to be a major risk or a life-altering event. Simply commit to pursue a goal or seek an achievement at which you're not guaranteed to succeed.

THIS WEEK'S SCRIPTURE MEMORY. Use the memory card at the back of the book to memorize this verse:

> *Fear not, for I am with you;*
> *Be not dismayed, for I am your God.*
> *I will strengthen you,*
> *Yes, I will help you,*
> *I will uphold you with My righteous right hand.*
> ISAIAH 41:10

ASSIGNMENT. Read week 1 and complete the activities before the next group experience. Consider going deeper into this content by reading chapter 4 in Dr. Jeremiah's book *What Are You Afraid Of?* (Tyndale, 2013).

Video sessions available for purchase at *www.lifeway.com/afraid*   **WEEK 1: DEFEAT**   9

OUR FIGHT AGAINST *MIGHT*

Do you realize how scary the word *might* can be? One primary source of our fear is the unknown quality of the future—the threat of what *might* happen. That's because fear trades in the market of possibility. It's the tyrant of the imagination, imposing itself on us from the shadows and from the hazy mirror of maybe.

My friend Don Wyrtzen knows what it's like to fear the unknown:

> The elusive monster of fear lurks in the shadows waiting to claw my soul to shreds. As one prone to melancholia, I see its ugly face often: when I'm struggling with the emotional stress of a difficult relationship, when I'm afraid failure is just around the corner, when success seems too hard to handle, and on days when free-floating anxiety is getting the best of me.[1]

I'm guessing you also understand the fearful potential of what *could* happen and what *might* be. I certainly do. Each week in this study, we'll focus on a specific element of that fearful potential—a specific threat of what *might* happen either today or in the future.

This week we'll look at the fear of failure. Or, in Don's words, we'll explore what to do "when I'm afraid failure is just around the corner."

This is a vital issue for today's culture. We live in a society that constantly defines us by our successes and continually drives us toward greater and greater accomplishments. How terrifying, then, to fail. How frightening to know that someday soon we'll trip and fall on our faces—and that everyone around us will see our defeat.

Here's the good news: we're not alone in our fear. This week we'll encounter a number of biblical characters who were forced to confront their fear of failure by turning to God as the guarantor of their success. Then we'll begin to understand what it takes for us to do the same.

1. Don Wyrtzen, *A Musician Looks at the Psalms* (Nashville: Broadman & Holman Publishers, 2004), 101.

DAY 1

FEAR NOT?

What are you afraid of? If you think that's a simple question, think again. Our fears are intricately connected with our deeper selves—our values, desires, and dreams. So evaluating what we're afraid of is a great way to learn more about who we really are.

To see what I mean, think for a few moments about the way you and your fears have changed over the years.

What were you most afraid of when you were a child? Record at least three answers.

1.

2.

3.

What are you most afraid of now?

What do your past and current fears reveal about your values, desires, and dreams?

Although some people actually like to feel afraid in controlled settings, such as a movie theater or a theme park, the vast majority of our experiences with fear are negative. Fear holds us back. It can defeat us before we even get started. It prevents us from achieving our goals and moving forward in both the short term and the long term.

So when I ask, "What are you afraid of?" I'm essentially asking, "What immobilizes you? What keeps you from experiencing a greater degree of success in life? What steals your joy and destroys your hope? What robs you of sleep night after night?"

On a spiritual level I'm asking, "What prevents you from entrusting your life wholly to a loving God who wants nothing but the best for you?"

I think I have a good idea of how you'd answer those questions—at least in part. That's because I've lived shoulder to shoulder with mature Christian people my entire life. I've also been a pastor for nearly five decades, and in that time I've discovered that everyone, myself included, is hindered by fear to one degree or another.

To what degree are you hindered by fear in your day-to-day life?

| 1 | 2 | 3 | 4 | 5 | 6 | 7 | 8 | 9 | 10 |

A small degree   A large degree

The good news is that we don't have to settle for paralysis. We can move beyond the fears that so often anchor us to mediocrity and stagnation in our Christian lives. And the first step in doing so is to understand what the Bible has to say about the specific fears that drag us down.

FEAR AND GOD'S WORD

The Bible has a lot to say about the subject of fear. At first glance, what the Bible says about fear can seem a little confusing—or at least a little contradictory.

On the one hand, the Scriptures command us more than three hundred times not to fear as we live our everyday lives. The phrase "fear not" is repeated throughout God's Word, including here:

> *Fear not, for I am with you;*
> *Be not dismayed, for I am your God.*
> *I will strengthen you,*
> *Yes, I will help you,*
> *I will uphold you with My righteous right hand.*
> ISAIAH 41:10

What's your initial reaction to this verse? Why?

In what ways have you seen God uphold you in times of fear?

On the other hand, the Scriptures are filled with men and women described as being afraid. And these weren't just the bad guys. Even biblical heroes like Moses, David, and Paul were afraid and were hindered by their fears. For example, look at what happened when Peter accepted an invitation to walk on water with Jesus:

> *When Peter had come down out of the boat, he walked on the water to go to Jesus. But when he saw that the wind was boisterous, he was afraid; and beginning to sink he cried out, saying, "Lord, save me!"*
> MATTHEW 14:29-30

When have you recently encountered a fearful situation? What happened?

There's an easy way to resolve this apparent contradiction. The heroes of the Bible were ordinary human beings who had to learn the same things you and I have to learn about fear. Specifically, they learned—

- to drive out fear by increasing their knowledge of God;
- to shift their focus away from their present fear and toward the eternal God;
- to trust God through faith instead of worrying about the future.

These are the practices we'll focus on in this study as we confront many of the major fears that often paralyze followers of Christ. We'll start this week with the fear of failure.

THE FEAR OF FAILURE

Some people suffer from a crippling fear of failure. I've known men and women who were so afraid of making a mistake that they were unable to take virtually any risks. And without taking risks, they were already defeated, unable to achieve ultimate success.

Most of us are affected by a less extreme version of this fear, but it still hinders us. All of us have had chances to leap for the brass ring and achieve something truly significant. But the fear of failure can keep us from even trying for success because we're afraid of what might happen—and who might see—if we miss the ring and fall.

When have you recently experienced failure while trying to accomplish something?

What emotions do you experience when you contemplate that failure?

Failure is by no means a modern invention, and neither is the fear of failure. Many people in the Bible experienced this fear, especially in the context of the call narratives.

If you're not familiar with that term, a *call narrative* is a passage of Scripture in which God called a person to engage in a particular task or assignment. For example, during the miraculous encounter with the burning bush, God called Moses to lead the Israelites out of slavery in Egypt. But Moses was so afraid of messing up that he almost missed the opportunity to join God's purpose:

> *Moses said to the LORD, "Oh, my Lord, I am not eloquent, either in the past or since you have spoken to your servant, but I am slow of speech and of tongue. Oh, my Lord, please send someone else."*
> EXODUS 4:10,13, ESV

Fortunately, God was patient with Moses and helped him overcome his fear. Indeed, one of the things I like about the call narratives is that they provide multiple opportunities for us to see how God responds with love to our fears and weaknesses.

Read Jeremiah 1:4-10. What do you learn about God from this passage?

Nowhere is God's concern for a fearful servant more evident than in the way He prepared Joshua to lead the children of Israel after the death of Moses (see Josh. 1). As we explore this account together this week, we'll see that God's encouragement of Joshua offers a clear, step-by-step strategy for dealing with the fear of failure in our lives today.

DAY 2

CONFRONTING FAILURE

Imagine the following scenarios. You're a recent MBA graduate suddenly asked to replace the beloved CEO of a thriving company. Or you're a rookie in the National Football League drafted by a team whose Hall-of-Fame quarterback retired in the offseason. Or you're a fledgling editor tasked with improving a new book by a best-selling author.

Get the point? Other people's success commonly triggers our fear of failure, especially when we know everyone will be watching our efforts and comparing our results with those of the previous regime. That's precisely the position in which Joshua found himself following the death of Moses.

What emotions do you experience when people around you excel?

How often do you compare your achievements with the achievements of others?

1	2	3	4	5	6	7	8	9	10
Not often									Very often

It's easy to make a case for Moses as one of the greatest men in history. Not only did he confront the most powerful man of his day and win, but he also led an entire nation out of slavery and served as the instrument for one of God's most impressive miracles in the parting of the Red Sea.

Most importantly, Moses had a unique relationship with God:

> *The LORD spoke to Moses face to face, as a man speaks to his friend. And he would return to the camp, but his servant Joshua the son of Nun, a young man, did not depart from the tabernacle.*
> EXODUS 33:11

Moses was a spiritual giant in his day, and Joshua was an eyewitness to everything Moses accomplished. Is it any wonder, then, that God felt it necessary to specifically encourage Joshua once he took Moses' place as the leader of God's people?

Read Joshua 1:1-9. How would you summarize these verses in a single sentence?

How do these verses contribute to your understanding of God?

I'd like us to dive deeper into these verses over the next couple of days. As we explore, we'll uncover six principles God used to help Joshua overcome the fear of failure. These principles are invaluable for helping us overcome our fear as well.

1. THE PRINCIPLE OF DIVINE PERSPECTIVE

God's words in Joshua 1:5 must have been very comforting to Joshua as a young leader:

> *As I was with Moses, so I will be with you. I will not leave you nor forsake you.*
> JOSHUA 1:5

God reminded Joshua of all the ways He'd led and provided for Moses, both during the exodus and throughout the wilderness. God promised to support Joshua as well and never to forsake him.

When have you felt most encouraged and supported by God?

At the same time, God reminded Joshua that He was the true source behind everything Moses accomplished. It was God who rescued the Israelites from the Egyptians. It was God who parted the Red Sea. It was God who brought the Israelites manna in the wilderness. God worked through Moses to accomplish incredible things, and He promised to do the same for Joshua.

How can you regularly remind yourself that God is the source of all your accomplishments?

Keeping that perspective in mind will encourage us when we might otherwise be overwhelmed by fear.

2. THE PRINCIPLE OF DIVINE PURPOSE

Having a purpose in life is one of the most wonderful feelings you can experience. Even if that purpose is temporary—even if it lasts only for a season—knowing what you're supposed to do in life brings tremendous comfort and focus.

That's the gift God gave Joshua:

> *Moses My servant is dead. Now therefore, arise, go over this Jordan, you and all this people, to the land which I am giving to them—the children of Israel. Every place that the sole of your foot will tread upon I have given you, as I said to Moses. From the wilderness and this Lebanon as far as the great river, the River Euphrates, all the land of the Hittites, and to the Great Sea toward the going down of the sun, shall be your territory.*
> JOSHUA 1:2-4

What are your initial reactions to these verses?

What ideas or images come to mind when you hear the word *purpose?* Why?

God blessed Joshua with a specific, achievable goal. He told His servant to go throughout the land of Canaan, an assignment that would require military confrontations and battles. Every place Joshua set his foot would be given to him and his people forever.

In essence, God helped Joshua focus on the task at hand. It's as if God said, "Even though Moses is gone and it seems as if the odds are stacked against you, I simply need you to commit to walk where I lead you. I'll take care of the rest."

When you encounter the fear of failure, combat that fear by regaining your God-given focus. The more focus, the less fear. And the less fear you experience, the less you'll experience failure.

> How would you describe your purpose in this season of your life?

> What steps can you take to focus more closely on that purpose in the coming weeks?

3. THE PRINCIPLE OF DIVINE PERSUASION

In addition to perspective and purpose, God knew Joshua needed some persuading. He needed to be prodded to move in the right direction. So God intentionally identified the character qualities His servant would need to fulfill his task:

> *Be strong and of good courage. ... Only be strong and very courageous. Be strong and of good courage; do not be afraid, nor be dismayed, for the LORD your God is with you wherever you go.*
> JOSHUA 1:6-7,9

These verses are the heart of God's motivational speech to His young servant. God knew strength and courage would be necessary for Joshua to persevere when times got tough. The good news for Joshua was that he'd already demonstrated strength and courage in the past.

> Read Numbers 14:5-9. How did Joshua demonstrate strength and courage in these verses?

Whom among your friends and family would you describe as strong and courageous?

Remember Joshua's strength and courage when you're confronted by the fear of failure. You can possess these qualities, just as Joshua did, if you take your fear to God and ask Him for what you need. Then put them into action on God's behalf, even if that leaves you in the minority.

When have you recently acted courageously in the face of opposition?

How did that experience change you?

How will you actively demonstrate courage when you feel afraid?

None of us like to be defeated while pursuing our goals, and each of us has been attacked by the fear of failure at one point or another. The key is to focus on God and seek His help in the midst of our fear, as Joshua did.

By maintaining a divine perspective, focusing on our divine purpose, and allowing God to point us in the right direction through divine persuasion, we can avoid paralysis and even gain ground when we're confronted by the fear of potential failure.

DAY 3

MOVING TOWARD SUCCESS

Probably the worst thing about the fear of failure is the way it subtly and surreptitiously prevents us from even attempting to reach our goals. The fear of being defeated sits quietly in the back of our minds, telling us over and over that we'll never win, and so we may as well not even try.

For that reason our first phase in combating the fear of failure is to shake loose from that paralysis and refuse to be stalled. Yesterday we examined three principles that can help us in that effort: the principle of divine perspective, the principle of divine purpose, and the principle of divine persuasion.

> How can following the previous principles help us break free from the paralysis caused by the fear of failure?

But shaking loose from our paralysis is only the first step in fighting the fear of failure. We also have to actively move toward success. It involves taking risks and taking action to accomplish what God expects of us each day as servants in His kingdom.

With that in mind, let's look at the final three principles God used to point Joshua toward success after Moses' death. As we do so, let's keep an eye open for specific ways we can use those principles to strive for success in our own lives.

> Review Joshua 1:1-9. What are some actions God commanded Joshua to take as the new leader of His people? Record at least three.

1.

2.

3.

4. THE PRINCIPLE OF DIVINE PRIORITY

As God prepared Joshua for a difficult leadership role, He didn't ask him to adopt a military strategy as his main concern. He didn't ask Joshua to focus on financial backing or bilateral relations with neighboring countries. Those skills certainly have a place and may have been helpful for Joshua, but they weren't his God-given priority.

Instead, God commanded Joshua to focus on His Word:

> *This Book of the Law shall not depart from your mouth, but you shall meditate in it day and night, that you may observe to do according to all that is written in it. For then you will make your way prosperous, and then you will have good success.*
> JOSHUA 1:8

What does it mean to meditate on God's Word?

What does it mean to observe God's Word?

How do you currently meditate on and observe the Bible during your normal routine?

Joshua's main priority was to contemplate, proclaim, and apply God's Word, which at the time was known as the Book of the Law. It included Genesis, Exodus, Leviticus, Numbers, and Deuteronomy. Those five books were Joshua's main path to taking action and achieving "good success" (v. 8) in his new role as the leader of God's people.

The same is true for us. The Bible is our launching pad for both encouragement and instruction when we want to throw off our fear of failure and strive for success.

How satisfied are you with your current efforts to study God's Word?

1	2	3	4	5	6	7	8	9	10

Not satisfied   Satisfied

What steps will you take to improve your study of the Bible in the coming weeks?

5. THE PRINCIPLE OF DIVINE PRESENCE

One thing that characterized Moses' life and ministry was the incredible level of access he had to God. Moses constantly sought and entered God's presence, and his time in God's presence changed him in profound ways:

> *Now it was so, when Moses came down from Mount Sinai (and the two tablets of the Testimony were in Moses' hand when he came down from the mountain), that Moses did not know that the skin of his face shone while he talked with Him. So when Aaron and all the children of Israel saw Moses, behold, the skin of his face shone, and they were afraid to come near him.*
>
> **EXODUS 34:29-30**

Moses' time in God's presence gave him more than a face that glowed in the dark. It made him secure in the knowledge that he didn't have to face any challenge or fear alone, because God was on his side.

It must have been deeply comforting, then, for Joshua to hear these words from God:

> *As I was with Moses, so I will be with you. I will not leave you nor forsake you. Be strong and of good courage; do not be afraid, nor be dismayed, for the LORD your God is with you wherever you go.*
>
> **JOSHUA 1:5,9**

What emotions do you experience when you read these verses? Why?

How do you currently spend time in God's presence?

It's important for us to understand that God didn't grant His presence only to Moses and Joshua. In fact, God consistently promised to remain with and support all of His servants, no matter what He called them to do or where He called them to go.

Read the following passages of Scripture and record God's promises.

Judges 6:16

Isaiah 41:8-10

Jeremiah 1:7-10

Here's the great news: this assurance extends to us as well through the incredible promise of Jesus after His resurrection from the dead:

> Go therefore and make disciples of all the nations, baptizing them in the name of the Father and of the Son and of the Holy Spirit, teaching them to observe all things that I have commanded you; and lo, I am with you always, even to the end of the age.
> MATTHEW 28:19-20

How will you intentionally rely on God's presence to deal with your fears in the coming weeks?

6. THE PRINCIPLE OF DIVINE PROSPERITY

God's final principle for Joshua includes two of the boldest and most encouraging statements in the entire Bible:

> No man shall be able to stand before you all the days of your life.
> JOSHUA 1:5

> This Book of the Law shall not depart from your mouth, but you shall meditate in it day and night, that you may observe to do according to all that is written in it. For then you will make your way prosperous, and then you will have good success.
> JOSHUA 1:8

The Hebrew word translated *success* means *to be prudent* or *to act circumspectly*. So in a religious and ethical sense, people who experience success are those who allow God to guide and direct their lives. Now notice the phrase "For then" in verse 8. The kind of success mentioned in this passage results from our willingness to value God's Word (the Book of the Law) so much that we read it, talk about it, meditate on it, and apply what it says in our everyday lives.

Joshua experienced that kind of success and prosperity throughout his time as the leader of God's people. Sure, he encountered hardships; sometimes he failed. But his journey through life was prudent, wise, and focused on serving God. Therefore, in God's eyes he was a success.

How do you define *success* in terms of your life and legacy?

How has God's Word influenced your understanding of success?

One of the best ways to combat the fear of failure is to take a risk, pursue a dream, and succeed. Once you get a taste of that kind of joy—that kind of accomplishment and affirmation of your purpose—you'll refuse to allow anything to hold you back.

What obstacles are currently preventing you from making further strides toward that kind of success?

What steps will you take in the short term and the long term to overcome those obstacles?

God offered six principles to help Joshua deal with and ultimately overcome the fear of failure. I know these principles work, because I've made them the core of my own walk with God. On many occasions, as I've faced the challenges of ministry and everyday life, these powerful words of God have given me the shot of courage I needed to push away from my paralysis and strive for the success God desires for my life. I pray you'll use these principles to do the same.

DAY 4

FEAR PROFILE: GIDEON

Fear strikes all types of people in the modern world. Old and young, large and small, wise and foolish, rich and poor, strong and weak—all of us face a wide variety of fears as we live, work, and play each day. This is true even for those of us who seek to advance the kingdom of God by serving Him.

Fear plagued many biblical characters as well. That's why I've chosen to include a fear profile in each week of this study. These profiles will help us focus on a specific servant of God and examine his confrontation with a potentially debilitating fear.

This week we've already concentrated on Joshua's fear of failure. We can also benefit by learning about Gideon, another man tasked with leading God's people through a difficult, dangerous situation.

GIDEON'S FEAR

Gideon was one of the judges who led the Israelites between the rule of Joshua and the reign of Saul, their first king. It's surprising, then, that Gideon is introduced in Scripture as a man frightened enough to literally hide from his enemies as part of his everyday routine.

> Read Judges 6:11-16. What are your initial impressions of Gideon from these verses?

> What do these verses teach us about God?

The Israelites had achieved stunning military and political success under the leadership of Moses and Joshua, but their situation had regressed in the years since they'd taken possession of the promised land. In fact, during Gideon's time the nation of Israel experienced heavy oppression at the hands of the Midianites. Things were so bad that Gideon was forced to thresh wheat inside a winepress, which prevented Midianite soldiers from seeing him and stealing his food (see v. 11).

Indeed, the situation was grim for Gideon and his fellow Israelites. But things seemed sure to change when God showed up with a promise of rescue:

> The Angel of the LORD appeared to him, and said to him, "The LORD is with you, you mighty man of valor! Go in this might of yours, and you shall save Israel from the hand of the Midianites. Have I not sent you?"
>
> JUDGES 6:12,14

What are the similarities between Gideon's call and the calls Moses (see Ex. 3:1-12) and Joshua experienced (see Josh. 1:1-9)?

This was an amazing opportunity for Gideon. Not only did he experience God in a unique and powerful way, but he was also offered an opportunity to achieve the kind of life-altering success modeled by Moses and Joshua—historical figures Gideon would have recognized and revered.

As we read this account, however, it's immediately clear that Gideon was driven not only by his fear of the Midianites but also by an overwhelming fear of failure:

> [Gideon] said to Him, "O my Lord, how can I save Israel? Indeed my clan is the weakest in Manasseh, and I am the least in my father's house."
>
> JUDGES 6:15

When have you recently felt unqualified for a task assigned to you? What happened next?

In what areas of life do you feel weak or underequipped? Record at least three.

1.

2.

3.

Gideon was so afraid of defeat that he asked God to wait around while he prepared an offering as a test to determine whether he was actually talking with God (see vv. 17-18). Then, when God passed the test by consuming the offering with fire (see vv. 19-22), Gideon was afraid he was going to die because he'd really seen God! Gideon was a man driven by fear.

GOD'S FAITHFULNESS

Fortunately for Gideon, God was faithful to support him through his many fears, including his fear of failure. Interestingly, God encouraged Gideon with many of the same principles and methods He'd used to help Moses and Joshua work through their fear of failure. For example, God used the principle of divine purpose to clearly and succinctly inform Gideon about his primary responsibility in what would become the most exciting season of his young life:

> *The LORD turned to him and said, "Go in this might of yours, and you shall save Israel from the hand of the Midianites. Have I not sent you?"*
>
> **JUDGES 6:14**

In addition, many of God's statements to Gideon reflect the principle of divine presence, including this one:

> *The LORD said to him, "Surely I will be with you, and you shall defeat the Midianites as one man."*
>
> **JUDGES 6:16**

God was incredibly patient with Gideon as the young leader adapted to living life in God's presence. Indeed, God chose to endure a *second* series of tests Gideon devised to determine whether God would really support him as the leader of the Israelites.

Read Judges 6:36-40. What do these verses teach you about Gideon?

What do these verses teach you about God?

When have you been tempted to test God's commitment to your well-being? What happened next?

Despite His patience with Gideon, God was by no means passive in His efforts to help the young leader achieve his potential. God had previously used the principle of divine persuasion to point Joshua in the right direction, and He took a similar path with Gideon. Specifically, God persuaded Gideon to trust Him alone by directing Gideon to dismiss the vast majority of his small army on the eve of battle with the Midianites:

> The LORD said to Gideon, "The people who are with you are too many for Me to give the Midianites into their hands, lest Israel claim glory for itself against Me, saying, 'My own hand has saved me.' Now therefore, proclaim in the hearing of the people, saying, 'Whoever is fearful and afraid, let him turn and depart at once from Mount Gilead.' " And twenty-two thousand of the people returned, and ten thousand remained.
> JUDGES 7:2-3

What's your initial reaction to this passage?

What was God teaching Gideon through this directive?

God said 10,000 soldiers were still too many, so He instructed Gideon to once again reduce the size of his army. When it was all said and done, Gideon was left with a fighting force of only 300 men (see Judg. 7:4-7). The end result was that Gideon was forced to trust God in order to face his fear and achieve success.

To what degree are you currently able to trust God when fearful challenges arise?

1	2	3	4	5	6	7	8	9	10
Unable to trust							Often able to trust		

What obstacles prevent you from trusting God to a greater degree?

It's important for us to understand that God didn't force Gideon into blind trust. He'd already given Gideon ample evidence of His power and faithfulness, and He still had more evidence to give:

> *It happened on the same night that the Lord said to him, "Arise, go down against the camp, for I have delivered it into your hand. But if you are afraid to go down, go down to the camp with Purah your servant, and you shall hear what they say; and afterward your hands shall be strengthened to go down against the camp."*
> JUDGES 7:9-11

Notice God's emphasis on the principle of divine prosperity. He promised Gideon success and victory in the upcoming battle. Also notice that God was aware of Gideon's continued fear. That's why He encouraged Gideon to take his servant to the enemy camp and listen to what the enemy soldiers had to say.

Here's what happened next:

> *When Gideon had come, there was a man telling a dream to his companion. He said, "I have had a dream: To my surprise, a loaf of barley bread tumbled into the camp of Midian; it came to a tent and struck it so that it fell and overturned, and the tent collapsed." Then his companion answered and said, "This is nothing else but the sword of Gideon the son of Joash, a man of Israel! Into his hand God has delivered Midian and the whole camp."*
> JUDGES 7:13-14

With this final burst of assurance, Gideon was able to overcome his fear of failure and achieve the level of success God desired for him. Will you do the same?

DAY 5

HOW TO PRIORITIZE GOD'S WORD

We've covered a lot of information this week about the fear of failure, and we'll cover a lot more over the course of this study as we explore many of the major fears that afflict people today. But information goes only so far. Learning is only the first step in the process of transformation. That's why I've set aside the last day of each week to focus on practical application. Once you've explored what the Bible says about a specific fear, I'd like you to make a plan or commit to an action step that will help you retain what you've learned and apply that information to eliminate your fear.

We've explored six principles this week, and each of them will be helpful in your efforts to overcome the fear of failure. But I want to focus on the principle of divine priority as our practical application today. That's because nothing will help you fight the fear of failure more than making the Bible a major priority in your life.

Of course, that's easier said than done in our world of busyness and constant change. So I'd like you to make a plan for prioritizing God's Word, and I'd like you to start by identifying the primary way you're currently hindered by the fear of failure.

> **What's your primary struggle with the fear of failure right now?**

Keep that struggle in mind as you work through the following pages and create action steps to fight the fear of failure through a proper prioritization of God's Word.

1. READ THE WORD OBEDIENTLY

The first step in prioritizing the Bible is to read it consistently. That's a vital discipline for anyone who chooses to follow Christ and live by the truths in God's Word. I love the way God phrased this discipline when speaking to Joshua, His servant:

> *Only be strong and very courageous, that you may **observe to do** according to all the law which Moses My servant commanded you. ... This Book of the Law shall not depart from your mouth, but you shall meditate in it day and night, that you may **observe to do** according to all that is written in it.*
> **JOSHUA 1:7-8, EMPHASIS ADDED**

That little phrase "observe to do" is especially valuable for us as Christians. Those three words remind us that we're not to read the Bible for information only. We're not to study the Bible simply so that we can know more. Instead, we're to study the Bible so that we can discover God's will for our lives. In other words, we're commanded to *observe* what the text says in order to *obey* the text as we live our lives.

> **Action step 1: Identify a verse we've studied this week that you'd like to claim for your fear of failure. What command or instruction is this verse asking you to obey?**

2. TALK ABOUT THE WORD CONSTANTLY

The next step in making God's Word a primary priority in your life is to talk about God's Word constantly. And I mean constantly. That's why God said this to Joshua:

> *This Book of the Law shall not depart from your mouth.*
> JOSHUA 1:8

That phrase "shall not depart from your mouth" doesn't mean Joshua was supposed to keep his jaws closed and never allow God's words to come out of his mouth—quite the opposite, actually. God wanted Joshua, as the leader of His people, to regularly and routinely talk about His Word. God wanted Joshua to be so saturated with the Scriptures that they permeated his conversations with other people.

That's what God wanted for Joshua in his devotion to the Word. God wants the same for us. We can fight against the fear of failure by making God's Word a priority, and one of the best ways to make God's Word a priority is for us to regularly and routinely talk about our experiences with it.

> **How often do you talk about the Bible and its contents with your friends and family?**
>
> 1   2   3   4   5   6   7   8   9   10
>
> Rarely   Daily

> **Action step 2: Set a goal of intentionally talking about the Bible with someone important in your life this week.**

3. MEDITATE ON THE WORD CONTINUALLY

God wanted the Book of the Law not only to permeate Joshua's conversations but also to regularly penetrate Joshua's inner thoughts:

> *This Book of the Law shall not depart from your mouth, but you shall meditate in it day and night, that you may observe to do according to all that is written in it.*
>
> JOSHUA 1:8

> What images or ideas come to mind when you hear the word *meditate*?

To meditate on something is to think deeply about it—to concentrate your mental energy on understanding and absorbing deeper truths. This discipline is vital for Christians today because we're constantly bombarded by cultural content ranging from trivial to dangerous.

To be frank, it's impossible to live in the world today and not have things spilled on us that we want no part of—images, ideas, and words. But those things don't have to affect us permanently. The Word of God acts like a stain-resistant coating for our hearts and minds. Meditating on the truths of Scripture helps us avoid the snares present in what we never meant to see or hear.

> Action step 3: Spend some time meditating on the verse you've chosen to address your fear. What is God teaching you through this verse?

4. FOLLOW THE WORD EXCLUSIVELY

Joshua 1:7 gives the next practical step for prioritizing the Bible in your life:

> *Only be strong and very courageous, that you may observe to do according to all the law which Moses My servant commanded you;* **do not turn from it to the right hand or to the left,** *that you may prosper wherever you go.*
>
> JOSHUA 1:7, EMPHASIS ADDED

When you commit to make God's Word a primary priority in your life, you must also commit to follow it exclusively. Don't turn to the right or left, allowing yourself to be influenced by false teachings and ideas. Rather, stay focused on the truth of Scripture.

Practically, that means we don't allow cultural or generational "wisdom" to influence our decisions when such wisdom contradicts the core truths of the Bible. That also means we don't compromise our interpretation of God's Word; we don't seek to make it politically correct on the one hand or overly judgmental and legalistic on the other. We don't proof-text by using isolated Scripture verses to justify our individual point of view. Instead, making the Bible a priority means submitting to God's law as our first and foremost source of authority.

> **Action step 4: Identify steps you will take to focus on God's truth in addressing your fear of failure this week.**

5. ACCEPT THE WORD TOTALLY

Making the Bible a major priority in your life requires making the *whole* Bible a priority in your life. Every page of God's Word is equally God's Word, and therefore every page of God's Word is vital to your life as a follower of God.

That's why God told Joshua not to observe and meditate on portions of the Scriptures in his day but on "all that is written in it" (Josh. 1:8). The same is true for you. Don't settle for lingering exclusively in the passages of Scripture with which you're most familiar. Rather, branch out. Explore. Experience the whole truth of God's Word.

> **Action step 5: Use a concordance or this week's study to find other verses that address your fear of failure. When will you intentionally study one of these passages to work against your fear of failure?**

It was no small thing that God called Joshua to focus on His Word, and it's no small thing that He calls us to do the same. The Bible is the greatest source of encouragement available today. When we read its truths, we're changed by its truths. We need His Word firmly implanted in our hearts and minds if we truly want to follow Him.

So whenever you experience the fear of failure and whenever you feel like a failure, turn to the Word of God. Find in the Bible the strong words that will lift you up and set you free from your fear, both now and in the future.

DEPRESSION: THE FEAR OF MENTAL BREAKDOWN

START

*WELCOME BACK TO THIS SMALL-GROUP DISCUSSION
OF* WHAT ARE YOU AFRAID OF?

The previous session's application challenge asked you to intentionally confront the fear of failure by taking a risk or attempting to achieve something at which you might fail. If you're comfortable, share your experiences by answering the following questions.

* What risk(s) did you take this week? What was the outcome?
* Describe the emotions you felt before, during, and after your experience(s) with taking risks.
* What have you learned about yourself this week?

What advice would you give to someone hindered by the fear of failure?

This session will focus on depression: the fear of mental breakdown. What ideas or images come to mind when you hear the word *depression?* Why?

To prepare for the DVD segment, read aloud the following verses.

> *After this Job opened his mouth and cursed the day of his birth. And Job spoke, and said:*
> *"May the day perish on which I was born,*
> *And the night in which it was said,*
> *'A male child is conceived.'*
> *May that day be darkness;*
> *May God above not seek it,*
> *Nor the light shine upon it."*
>
> JOB 3:1-4

WATCH

COMPLETE THE VIEWER GUIDE BELOW AS YOU WATCH DVD SESSION 2.

Depression: low spirits, gloomy feelings, dejection, _____, a condition marked by feelings of _____, failure, and accompanying guilt

THE EPIDEMIC OF DEPRESSION
More than _____ in _____ American adults are treated for depression during their lives.

Major depression is the leading cause of _____ worldwide.

An estimated _____ _____ people worldwide suffer from depression.

THE EXPERIENCE OF DEPRESSION
Depression is a human problem, a fact of life that shouldn't _____ us.

THE EXPRESSION OF DEPRESSION
Job 3

THE EXAMINATION OF DEPRESSION
_____ people sometimes get depressed.

THE EXPLANATIONS OF DEPRESSION
1. _____ reasons   2. _____ reasons

   It is very difficult to feel well emotionally, mentally, and spiritually when you are feeling awful _____.

3. _____ reasons   4. _____ reasons

THE ELIMINATION OF DEPRESSION
1. _____ it.   2. _____ it.

3. _____ it.   4. _____ it.

THE EFFECT OF DEPRESSION
Job 23:10

RESPOND

USE THE FOLLOWING QUESTIONS TO DISCUSS THE DVD SEGMENT WITH YOUR GROUP.

What did you appreciate most in Dr. Jeremiah's teaching?

What is an appropriate definition of *depression?*

How would you summarize our culture's reaction to the epidemic of depression?

How would you summarize the church's reaction to the epidemic of depression?

Respond to Dr. Jeremiah's statement: "The reality is that godly believers sometimes get depressed. Depression has been called the common cold of the soul, for sooner or later most people catch it. And God's servants, including Job, are not immune."

How should we as individuals face and fight depression?

How can we as a group support and encourage those among us who face depression?

APPLICATION. Spend time increasing your knowledge of depression this week. For example, read an article by a psychologist, talk with someone who helps treat depression, or watch a movie on the subject. Be prepared to briefly discuss your findings at the next group experience.

THIS WEEK'S SCRIPTURE MEMORY. Use the memory card at the back of the book to memorize this verse:

> *The LORD, He is the One who goes before you. He will be with you, He will not leave you nor forsake you; do not fear nor be dismayed.*
> DEUTERONOMY 31:8

ASSIGNMENT. Read week 2 and complete the activities before the next group experience. Consider going deeper into this content by reading chapter 8 in Dr. Jeremiah's book *What Are You Afraid Of?* (Tyndale, 2013).

SPIRITUAL CANCER

Here's an interesting question. Could the United States be the world's saddest nation? Statistics from the World Health Organization and Harvard Medical School suggest that could indeed be the case.

A recent study conducted by those organizations found that 9.6 percent of Americans experience bipolar disorder, major depressive disorder, or chronic minor depression over the course of a given year. That's the highest percentage among the 14 major nations polled. Interestingly, many of the nations that received better scores than the United States are currently suffering from war, serious unemployment, and poverty—nations such as Lebanon, Mexico, and Nigeria.[1]

Based on the results of this study, the chances are good that you know someone who regularly struggles with depression. The chances are also good that you've struggled with depression in your own life or that you'll face that struggle sometime in the future.

Sadly, Christians often fail to understand that depression is the spiritual equivalent of cancer or another terrible illness. The difference is that because depression comes from within, we often fail to recognize it. We only know we're confused and frightened by the gradual changes we perceive in our loved ones or in ourselves.

For all of these reasons I strongly believe we as Christians need to talk about the fear of depression. I know it's a difficult subject; what's more depressing than thinking deeply about depression? But this is an illness that no longer affects a relatively small sample of our population. As we'll see this week, depression is a spiritual epidemic in our country and around the world. Yet believers can confront this epidemic by using both spiritual and practical principles.

Even in the throes of despondency, a follower of Christ always has hope. This week's study will explore depression not only as a major source of fear but also as a major opportunity to move closer to God and advance His kingdom on earth.

1. Bret Stephens, "The Great Depression," *Wall Street Journal,* March 9, 2007.

DAY 1

DEFINING *DEPRESSION*

One Sunday morning in 1857 the famous British preacher C. H. Spurgeon shocked his five thousand listeners when he stood up in the Music Hall, Royal Surrey Gardens, to begin a sermon from Isaiah 41:14. Here's what he said:

> *I have to speak to-day to myself; and whilst I shall be endeavoring to encourage those who are distressed and down-hearted, I shall be preaching, I trust to myself, for I need something which shall cheer my heart—Why I can not tell, wherefore I do not know, but I have a thorn in the flesh, a messenger of Satan to buffet me; my soul is cast down within me, I feel as if I had rather die than live; all that God hath done by me seems to be forgotten, and my spirit flags and my courage breaks down. ... I need your prayers.*[1]

I'm sure some people in that congregation found it incomprehensible that the world's greatest preacher would confess to such despair. But I'm equally sure many others understood what Spurgeon was feeling and saying, because depression has always been more prevalent than most people think.

What ideas or images come to mind when you hear the word
depression? **Why?**

When have you recently encountered depression in your life
or in the lives of others?

As we'll see this week, depression is certainly a frightening consequence of our fallen status as human beings. But it doesn't have to define us or distract us from our purpose in life. In fact, when faced correctly, depression provides a unique opportunity for us to glorify our good God in the midst of our challenging circumstances.

THE EPIDEMIC OF DEPRESSION

Earlier I mentioned that depression is more common than most people realize, and that's true. But the grim reality is that depression has reached epidemic levels. The raw numbers are startling:

- In the United States the lifetime risk of developing major depression is around 17 percent.[2]
- Nearly 17 million American adults and 2 million teens report major depression each year.[3]
- Depression is the leading cause of disability in the United States for ages 15 to 44.[4]
- The use of antidepressants has soared nearly 400 percent since 1988; antidepressants are now the most commonly prescribed medication for young adults.[5]

Depression is a widespread sickness in modern society that's only getting worse.

What's your initial reaction to the previous statistics?

Where do you see the consequences of depression in society?

I've occasionally experienced discouragement during my life, but to the best of my knowledge, I've never crossed the line into depression. However, because I'm a pastor, I've counseled many people trapped in the darkness of depression, and I've thoroughly researched the affliction in order to help them.

The more time I've spent with depressed people, the more I've noticed common themes and experiences: empty hearts, lifeless spirits, and a sadness that recurs like cancer. The dust of death comes through the words of depressed people, and I've come to realize there's no deeper disease of the soul.

I've also realized that fear is intimately connected with depression. Because most people's fears are identifiable, they can be resisted and repelled. But when depression is involved, the fears can't be grasped and fought. They capture their target and won't let go.

What do you find most troubling about the epidemic of depression in the world today? Why?

Thankfully, there are things we can do to keep our spirits healthy, just as we can exercise to maintain our physical health. And although it's appropriate and necessary to reach out for help during times of darkness, we'll be more likely to find healing in the future if we proactively care for our souls in the present.

The first course of action in combatting depression and the fear of depression is to know our enemy. Several characters in the Bible show us what it's like to be depressed and what's required to be healed. We can start by learning from them.

THE EXPERIENCE OF DEPRESSION

Let's begin with a definition. To depress something simply means to make it lower than it normally is. In this sense everybody has experienced some form of depression at various points in life. All of us have had low points in our physical, emotional, and spiritual lives.

How often do you experience spiritual or emotional low moments?

1	2	3	4	5	6	7	8	9	10
Rarely									Frequently

How do you typically recover from these low moments?

The illness known as clinical depression is something different and far more serious than these low points in life. People who are clinically depressed have a very difficult time moving out of the low periods on their own. For these individuals, depression soaks through flesh and bone, shadows the mind, and even quenches the human spirit.

Because we are holistic beings, depressed people suffer not just in spirit but also in body. They become ill more often. They lose the energy they need for everyday life and fall into lethargy or escape into sleep when it can be found. They struggle to think clearly and to care about anything around them.

Here's something I need to make clear: depression isn't a secular affliction. It's a *human* affliction that can strike all people, regardless of their spiritual state. Many Christian heroes through the ages, as well as many Christians in the church today, have suffered from bouts of depression. So depression doesn't indicate a lack of spirituality.

The Bible also contains several case studies of men and women who experienced depression. Look at Moses, for example, who was tasked with leading a whining nation of Israelites on an aimless journey through the desert:

> *I am not able to bear all these people alone, because the burden is too heavy for me. If You treat me like this, please kill me here and now—if I have found favor in Your sight—and do not let me see my wretchedness!*
> **NUMBERS 11:14-15**

That kind of "Kill me now" mentality recurred in the story of Elijah, when the prophet was hounded and pursued by the wicked Queen Jezebel:

> *[Elijah] himself went a day's journey into the wilderness, and came and sat down under a broom tree. And he prayed that he might die, and said, "It is enough! Now, Lord, take my life, for I am no better than my fathers!"*
> **1 KINGS 19:4**

Where do you see depression reflected in the previous verses?

In a similar way, David's psalms record eloquent expressions of depression and despair.

Read the following passages and record how they reflect David's struggle with depression.

Psalm 22:1-8

Psalm 42:1-8

Psalm 143:1-8

Depression is an issue we must take seriously as individuals and as a church. Many people fear both the potential depression carries for disruption and the reality of what they've already experienced—and that's understandable. The specter of depression is genuinely terrifying.

Let's remember, however, that no situation is hopeless. Whether you worry about the possibility of depression or have already experienced the darkness, I promise that you can find the light. In fact, remember how both Moses and Elijah despaired to the point of wishing they could die? Thankfully, that wasn't the end of their stories. They went on to serve God faithfully. In fact, their stories didn't end even with their physical deaths:

> *After six days Jesus took Peter, James, and John his brother, led them up on a high mountain by themselves; and He was transfigured before them. His face shone like the sun, and His clothes became as white as the light. And behold, Moses and Elijah appeared to them, talking with Him.*
> MATTHEW 17:1-3

As Christians, we also have the privilege of meeting with Jesus. And we're blessed by the One who said these words:

> *I am the light of the world. He who follows Me shall not walk in darkness, but have the light of life.*
> JOHN 8:12

> **How has Jesus encouraged and uplifted you during the low moments of your life?**

Jesus Christ is the ultimate antidote for both depression and the fear of depression. While there are other legitimate ways to combat those afflictions, He is our Light in the midst of darkness, and we ultimately depend on Him.

DAY 2

EXPLORING DEPRESSION

We've already explored several examples of individuals in Scripture who experienced depression, but I don't think there's a more poignant expression of depression than the account recorded in Job 3. You're probably familiar with the story. Job was a deeply spiritual man who'd experienced the fullness of life's blessings. He was wealthy and successful. He was married and the loving father of several children. He was respected in the community and enjoyed an especially intimate relationship with God.

Until the day it all came crashing down.

> Read Job 1:13-22; 2:1-10. What are your initial reactions to these passages of Scripture?

> What emotions do you typically experience when you lose something or someone you love?

The remaining chapters of the Book of Job paint an emotional portrait of the human struggle against depression. What started as the collapse of Job's external life—wealth, family, and health—became a battle to prevent his inner life from collapsing as well. As long as we maintain faith and hope, losses can be restored. But when depression sets in, faith and hope are often cut loose. When those anchors of the soul are gone, it's hard for people who suffer from deep despair to rise up and reverse their situations.

That's why Job was paralyzed for much of his story, unable to do anything except profess his innocence and ask why. In Job 3 we see a bold display of Job's humanity as he poured out three laments to God.

We've examined depression and the fear of depression in a general way, but now let's explore each of Job's laments to gain a better understanding of how depression affects us as individuals—as real people who need help.

"WHY DID I ARRIVE?"

Job's first lament arrived with a curse. He didn't curse God as his wife suggested (see Job 2:9), but he did curse the day he was born:

> *After this Job opened his mouth and cursed the day*
> *of his birth.*
> *And Job spoke, and said:*
> *"May the day perish on which I was born,*
> *And the night in which it was said,*
> *'A male child is conceived.'*
> *May that day be darkness;*
> *May God above not seek it,*
> *Nor the light shine upon it."*
> JOB 3:1-4

These were the words of a man who saw no future for himself. This was plain, ugly honesty—the speech of a wounded soul.

Was it wrong for Job to express these feelings to God? Explain.

How do you typically express bitterness and frustration when you feel them most keenly?

We all know what it's like when deep anguish finds its voice inside us. When life becomes irrational, our point of view follows suit, and we say things we might never have imagined. That's one element of depression that makes it so frightening.

"WHY DID I SURVIVE?"

Not only did Job curse the day of his birth, but he also questioned the meaning of the life made possible through that birth:

Why did I not die at birth?
Why did I not perish when I came from the womb?
Or why was I not hidden like a stillborn child,
Like infants who never saw light?
There the wicked cease from troubling,
And there the weary are at rest.
JOB 3:11,16-17

Read Job 3:11-19. How would you summarize Job's expressions in this passage?

When life is good, we appreciate the everyday blessings that give meaning to our existence—the rewards of work, the laughter of children, the sun on our face. But when all those joys are stripped away, we quickly forget what we've experienced. We quickly convince ourselves that life has always been as dark and meaningless as it feels in the moment of depression.

We later learn in Job's story that he still hoped for redemption by the hand of God (see Job 19:25-27). But caught in the moment of depression, Job was unable to identify anything meaningful about his past experiences. He felt his life had been a waste.

That's another frightening element of depression: it keeps us from remembering even the good times in our lives. It robs us of what we need when we need it most.

What have been some of the most meaningful blessings in your life?

How can you preserve your appreciation of those blessings in order to remember them during times of despondency?

"WHY AM I ALIVE?"

Job's third lament represents a common theme in today's culture. He wanted to know why he couldn't simply give up and pass away:

> *Why is light given to him who is in misery,*
> *And life to the bitter of soul,*
> *Who long for death, but it does not come,*
> *And search for it more than hidden treasures;*
> *Who rejoice exceedingly,*
> *And are glad when they can find the grave?*
> JOB 3:20-22

In the same way Job was unable to find comfort or meaning in the blessings of his past, he felt hopeless about the purpose underpinning his future. He simply wanted to give up and stop hurting.

How have you seen this hopeless aspect of depression reflected in our society?

What's important to remember is that Job *didn't* give up. He kept fighting for his life. Even when he no longer understood his purpose, even when he held no hope for light and laughter in the future, Job trusted God enough to hang on and cling to the Savior as his only hope. Later he was able to affirm:

> *I know that my Redeemer lives,*
> *And He shall stand at last on the earth;*
> *And after my skin is destroyed, this I know,*
> *That in my flesh I shall see God.*
> JOB 19:25-26

Know this: veterans of despair have a place in God's kingdom. Like Job, when we feel lost in the darkness, we must simply hold on in faith to the knowledge that God is good and desires good for us. We must remember that God has an eternal purpose for our lives, even if the present moment is filled with sorrow.

DAY 3

EXPLAINING DEPRESSION

If you've ever raised children or been around children for a significant period of time, you know what it's like when children go through the *why* phase. This is a particular stage in development when kids seem to ask the question *why* as many times as they possibly can each day.

Most children eventually grow out of this phase. Indeed, I've observed that many adults have reached the point where they feel uncomfortable asking why. This is especially true in our relationship with God. We often feel it's sinful or inappropriate to question God about His motives.

How do you feel in general about asking why?

Do you think it's appropriate to ask God why in connection with His plans for your life? Explain.

The truth is that it's never a sin to ask why, even of God. In Job 3, for example, Job looked to the heavens seven times and asked why. Even Jesus asked why as He was dying on the cross (see Matt. 27:46).

The only potential danger with the *why* question is when we begin to demand that God answer it—when we act as if He owes us a response. Such a demand isn't appropriate. Instead, we must humbly maintain our faith and trust in God even when He's silent.

What emotions do you experience when you feel that God is silent?

As Job's drama played out, we have the benefit of a backstage pass. We understand more than Job himself did about why these things were happening. We've been clued in to the spiritual undercurrents that brought on the storm in his life.

Unfortunately, we almost never have the same information in our own lives, especially about depression. We don't know the details of any spiritual warfare surrounding us, and we're often unaware of the chemical or emotional foundations that undergird our depression. Sometimes the night clutches its mysteries and holds them tightly.

Still, there are some common elements that regularly contribute to the experience of depression in our lives. Educating ourselves about the most common reasons for depression can allay some of our fears and can guide us to solutions.

SITUATIONAL CAUSES

Sometimes specific, identifiable circumstances drive us toward depression. That was certainly the case with Job. The sudden loss of his family, his wealth, and his health shocked him and sent him tumbling into ever-increasing darkness.

Another biblical character who experienced situational triggers for depression was David. These typically took the form of oppression by his enemies:

> *Vindicate me, O God,*
> *And plead my cause against an ungodly nation;*
> *Oh, deliver me from the deceitful and unjust man!*
> *Why are you cast down, O my soul?*
> *And why are you disquieted within me?*
> PSALM 43:1,5

When you find yourself moving toward depression, it's always a good idea to try and take a step back for self-evaluation. Ask yourself questions like these: *What challenges am I facing? In what ways have I been hurt? How am I feeling unfulfilled?*

How would you answer the previous questions?

Whom can you rely on to help you assess your circumstances when you begin feeling low?

SYSTEMIC CAUSES

I've heard it said that our souls and our bodies live so close together that they catch each other's diseases. Physical damage can cause us to receive spiritual and emotional damage and vice versa. So it's no surprise that disease and other physical traumas are major triggers for depression in our lives.

How have you experienced the connection between your physical health and your spiritual and emotional well-being?

I especially appreciate the words of Dr. Martyn Lloyd-Jones on this matter. As a medical doctor and prominent preacher, he observed much about the connection between the body and the spirit during his 30 years of service at Westminster Chapel in London:

> There are many, I find, who come to talk to me about these matters, in whose case it seems quite clear to me that the cause of the trouble is mainly physical. Into this group, speaking generally, you can put tiredness, overstrain, illness, any form of illness. You cannot isolate the spiritual from the physical for we are body, mind and spirit. The greatest and the best Christians when they are physically weak are more prone to an attack of spiritual depression than at any other time and there are great illustrations of this in the Scriptures.[6]

What steps can you take to prevent physical problems from triggering spiritual and emotional problems?

SATANIC CAUSES

Earlier I mentioned that we readers have access to the backstory of Job's drama. And a major part of that backstory includes the accusations and attacks of Satan.

Read Job 1:6-12. What are your initial reactions to this passage?

Read Job 2:1-6. What do these passages teach us about Satan?

What do these passages teach us about God?

Satan's twofold attack of Job is the clearest instance in Scripture that shows Satan intentionally hounding someone into despair. In the New Testament the apostle Paul experienced a similar attack, but the results were much different:

Lest I should be exalted above measure by the abundance of the revelations, a thorn in the flesh was given to me, a messenger of Satan to buffet me, lest I be exalted above measure.
2 CORINTHIANS 12:7

We don't know who or what this "messenger" was, but we know God gave Paul the grace he needed to endure Satan's attack (see vv. 8-9). We can safely say God's grace preserved Job as well. The difference between their responses was due to the fact that Job didn't understand the satanic cause of the affliction, while Paul did.

Believers today need to stay alert to Satan's attacks as well. His ultimate goal isn't to destroy our property or our bodies but our faith in God. If satanic attack underlies our depression, we need to remember that we have access to the same grace and power that sustained Job and Paul.

Thankfully, Jesus Himself showed us how to deal with satanic attacks.

Read Matthew 4:1-11. How would you describe Jesus' defense against Satan's attacks?

The sword of the Spirit—the Word of God—is the one offensive weapon in the Christian's spiritual armor (see Eph. 6:17). In times of spiritual warfare, it's the only way to counter the lies Satan always tells (see John 8:44).

SPIRITUAL CAUSES

The final cause of depression I'd like to mention is the one that feels most troubling to many people: there are times when God allows or even initiates the suffering and hardship that lead to depression in our lives. I once heard an old preacher say it this way: "God sometimes puts his children to bed in the dark."[7]

What's your response to the idea that God allows or even initiates suffering in our lives?

Read Job 42:1-6. How would you summarize Job's response to God at the end of his suffering?

Through his pain Job learned an important lesson that the Bible makes abundantly clear: God is in charge. Job's suffering was more spiritual than physical. His depression stemmed more from his unanswered questions than from his loss of property, children, and health. Although God never answered Job's questions, Job learned that God was all-powerful, all-knowing, and far beyond his ability to understand. When Job gained a proper perspective of God, he returned to a place of peace and prosperity (see v. 12).

In other words, he decided to let God be God.

In what areas of your life do you need to let God be God today?

Depression can arise for any or all of the four reasons we've explored today and more. The good news comes when we understand, as Job eventually did, that we need not comprehend the darkness in order to recover the light.

DAY 4

FEAR PROFILE: ELIJAH

Do you remember Elijah's showdown with the prophets of Baal on Mount Carmel? A lone voice for the supremacy of God, Elijah challenged Ahab, the king of Israel, and 450 prophets of Baal to a divine grudge match. He concocted a test designed to find out once and for all whether Baal or Yahweh was the true God.

As you might imagine, the results weren't even close.

> **Read 1 Kings 18:20-40. What do you enjoy most about this passage?**

Elijah's triumph stands as one of the more impressive spiritual victories in Scripture. It revealed the tremendous faith Elijah placed not only in God but also in God's power and authority over all creation. That's why it's so surprising to see what happened next.

When Queen Jezebel became furious over the death of her prophets and promised to have Elijah killed, he fled in terror. In spite of God's overwhelming provision during the earlier confrontation with the prophets of Baal, Elijah abandoned his God-given post and "ran for his life" into the wilderness (1 Kings 19:3).

As a result, Elijah experienced an acute bout of depression:

> *He himself went a day's journey into the wilderness, and came and sat down under a broom tree. And he prayed that he might die, and said, "It is enough! Now, Lord, take my life, for I am no better than my fathers!"*
>
> **1 KINGS 19:4**

Elijah's rapid descent into depression is jarring, given his earlier triumph. But his story allows us to explore two key steps we can take to fight against depression and the many fears associated with it.

1. FIND HELP

Sometimes we simply can't handle the darkness and the fear of depression on our own. Despite our best efforts and despite our personal pride, we sometimes need to reach out for help. And that really is OK.

Even if we don't have the strength to search for help, we need to keep the presence of mind and the humility to accept the help God and others provide. That's the only way Elijah was able to make it:

> As he lay and slept under a broom tree, suddenly an angel touched him, and said to him, "Arise and eat." Then he looked, and there by his head was a cake baked on coals, and a jar of water. So he ate and drank, and lay down again. And the angel of the LORD came back the second time, and touched him, and said, "Arise and eat, because the journey is too great for you." So he arose, and ate and drank; and he went in the strength of that food forty days and forty nights as far as Horeb, the mountain of God.
>
> 1 KINGS 19:5-8

When have you felt that "the journey [was] too great for you" (v. 7)?

How do you typically respond when others offer to help you during a time of need?

Elijah was exhausted. He was physically and emotionally spent—maxed out to the point of breaking. But with some food and a lot of rest, he was able to continue the journey.

Please don't overlook Elijah's experience in that wilderness. We live in a world that's always busy and bustling. There are always things to do, obstacles to break down, and goals to achieve. But we all need rest. We all need a break every now and then to recharge, just as Elijah did.

In fact, rest is so important to our experience as human beings that our Heavenly Father has commanded us to find it at least once a week (see Ex. 20:8-10).

What obstacles most often keep you from experiencing regular periods of rest?

In a given week how often do you intentionally set aside a significant amount of time for rest?

1	2	3	4	5	6	7	8	9	10

Almost never   Regularly

Notice that Elijah's period of rest wasn't a permanent solution to his depression. The ability to rest simply allowed him to keep going on his journey to find the help he needed most.

2. FIND GOD

God is the ultimate antidote for both depression and the fear of depression. That doesn't mean we shouldn't seek help in other ways, including counseling and a doctor's care. But God is the ultimate Light who can guide us through the darkness.

That's what Elijah discovered at the end of his journey.

> Read 1 Kings 19:9-18. What can we learn about Elijah from these verses?

> What can we learn about God from these verses?

Elijah had two opportunities to speak with God, and both times he chose to vent the confusion and bitterness that had driven him to emotional despair:

> *I have been very zealous for the Lord God of hosts; for the children of Israel have forsaken Your covenant, torn down Your altars, and killed Your prophets with the sword. I alone am left; and they seek to take my life.*
> 1 KINGS 19:10; ALSO SEE VERSE 14

Again, we need to understand that it's entirely appropriate for us to express our pain and confusion to God. Elijah took advantage of that opportunity, just as Job did, and we can do the same. But in the context of these verses, God's responses to Elijah are far more helpful and informative than the prophet's complaints.

God responded to the first complaint by instructing Elijah to wait for a period of time—something we must become accustomed to even in the midst of depression—and then He allowed the prophet to experience His presence. In other words, God blessed Elijah through an intimate encounter with Himself. This was an incredible gift!

How do you currently seek and savor time in God's presence?

God's response to Elijah's second complaint was fascinating:

> *The Lord said to him: "Go, return on your way to the Wilderness of Damascus; and when you arrive, anoint Hazael as king over Syria. Also you shall anoint Jehu the son of Nimshi as king over Israel. And Elisha the son of Shaphat of Abel Meholah you shall anoint as prophet in your place.*
> 1 KINGS 19:15-16

Basically, God told Elijah to get back to work. The prophet had expressed his frustration and despair and had received comfort through God's "still small voice" (v. 12). But there came a time when Elijah needed to take the focus off himself and return to the ministry God had given him.

What are the primary areas of ministry through which God has called you to serve Him and others?

I don't know what you're experiencing now in terms of depression, and I don't know what seasons of despair will come in your future. But I'm certain you can learn from the story of Elijah. When life turns dark, we need to seek the presence of God, our Light. And when we've received comfort from His still small voice, we need to continue the work of sharing His light with the rest of the world.

DAY 5

HOW TO FIGHT DEPRESSION

In his book *Depression* Edward Welch points out that it's the ending of a story that determines our ultimate experience with that story. *Romeo and Juliet* is a lovely romance until it all comes to a tragic conclusion. Other stories are almost painful until everything comes together in a happy ending. We stay on the edge of our seats at a movie because we're uncertain what will happen.

But what if we see the same film again? Now we know the plot. The complications and misunderstandings and entanglements don't fool us. We know where it's all headed. Sure, things may look gloomy right now, but just wait! The faces around us are filled with worry, but we wear confident smiles. We *know*.[8]

Life is like that for those who know God. We've read the Book. We know the ending. And though there are plot entanglements and complications, though we have our laughs and shed genuine tears, we know how it all works out. We can't lose. God's love wins the victory. Those who trust Him will live happily ever after. End of story.

So yes, times of deep sorrow will come. There will be times when we find ourselves lost and wandering, and the sky will grow dark. But even then, even in the most difficult moments, we can remember that we know the end of this plot.

Christ has the last word. And it's all right for us to cry sometimes because we know at the end of the road, He waits to dry every tear (see Rev. 21:4).

> **Read Revelation 21:1-8. How can you actively focus on the end of your story as you live, work, and minister in your day-to-day life?**

Having said all that, we can still be practical when it comes to preventing the dark times in our lives and to breaking free from the darkness when it arrives. So let's conclude this week's study by exploring four principles that can help us avoid the tendency toward deep, lasting emotional distress. In addition, these principles can help us deal with the pain and frustration of depression when it finds us.

1. REVEAL YOUR DEPRESSION

Have you heard the expression "Honesty is the best policy"? That's a true and powerful statement when it comes to spiritual and emotional distress.

When we experience pain or difficult circumstances, our instincts often drive us to hide the feelings that come with it—feelings like confusion, frustration, bitterness, anger, and despair. But it's the decision to bury our feelings that so often allows them to fester and turn into depression.

In a given month how often do you share your deeper feelings with another person?

1   2   3   4   5   6   7   8   9   10

Rarely   Often

Job was a superb model of transparency. He filled the ears of his friends with his intense feelings and deeper questions:

> *I will not restrain my mouth;*
> *I will speak in the anguish of my spirit;*
> *I will complain in the bitterness of my soul.*
> JOB 7:11

Our greatest error in the face of depression is to privatize our pain. When we reveal our confusion and despair to those who care about us, including our Heavenly Father, we take an important step in breaking the downward spiral toward depression.

In what ways are you currently being affected by negative emotions or painful circumstances?

Action step 1: Identify at least three trustworthy persons with whom you can share deeper feelings and negative emotions when needed.

1.

2.

3.

2. RESIST YOUR DEPRESSION

When Jesus encountered a lame man lying beside the pool at Bethesda, He asked a seemingly obvious question: "Do you want to be made well?" (John 5:6). But Jesus' query wasn't obvious, nor was it rhetorical.

Nobody wants to be sick, and certainly none of us desire to be depressed. But when we experience afflictions and negative circumstances, we need to consider how intent we are on being healed. The reality is that depression distorts our feelings and stifles our desires, including our desire for wholeness. Distress can become the new normal, causing us to lose our vision of ordinary happiness.

Therefore, we must choose to fight. When we're confronted with depression or with negative emotions and difficult circumstances that often lead to depression, one of the most important steps we can take is the firm decision to actively resist the darkness.

> What steps have you recently taken to fight for your physical wellness and well-being?

> What are some steps you can take in the near future to fight for your emotional and mental well-being?

> Action step 2: Choose one of the previous steps and commit to follow through with that step this week.

3. RESEARCH YOUR DEPRESSION

Earlier in the week we identified four common explanations for depression: situational, systemic, satanic, and spiritual causes. This isn't an exhaustive list, of course, and all of us as individuals are unique in terms of how we're affected by different situations.

Therefore, one way you can actively resist depression is to research yourself and your specific circumstances. Take a moment to examine your Christian life and determine whether you've slowly, imperceptibly stopped doing some of the things that healthy Christians do. In the same way, research your physical health, emotional experiences, intellectual pursuits, and so on.

Basically, you know better than anyone how you function best and what normal is like in your life. So you're eminently qualified to give yourself a regular checkup as a way to resist the destructive influence of depression.

> Action step 3: Give yourself a checkup by evaluating whether any of the following causes are currently pushing you toward depression.
>
> Jarring or painful situations:
>
> Physical illness or trauma:
>
> Spiritual warfare or oppression:
>
> Test or trial initiated by God:
>
> Other possible causes:

4. REPLACE YOUR DEPRESSION

If God is the ultimate Light that can lead us out of darkness, then the best way for us to combat depression is to replace our negative experiences with positive encounters in His presence. We must turn to God.

I'll warn you that turning to God and seeking His presence may not always go the way we anticipate. It's been my experience that as we tell God what we *want*, He gives us what we *need*. We frequently don't know what to pray for, but God is gracious and kind, holding higher standards for us than we have for ourselves.

Job came to God because he desperately wanted answers to his questions; he wanted to understand why so many bad things had happened to him. In a similar way, Paul turned to God in search of relief from his "thorn in the flesh" (2 Cor. 12:7).

In both of those situations, God had the grace to give His children what they truly needed—more of Himself. And He will do the same for us. The blessings He brings are seldom what we expected, but they're always better than we could have dreamed.

When have you been most blessed and satisfied by time spent in God's presence?

Action step 4: How will you actively and intentionally seek God's presence this week?

I like the way Mike Mason summarized the importance of Job's story in God's Word:

> Just the presence in Scripture of a book so dark, chaotic, and thoroughly eccentric as *Job* should come as an immense comfort to any suffering believer. For the book says, in effect, "This is what faith is often like. Do not be surprised if you find yourself confused, doubting, afflicted, all but crushed. It does not mean you have lost favor with God."[9]

Depression is a serious affliction that produces fear even in the strongest of God's children. But even in the darkest moments we're still His children. Even when things seem hopeless, we need to hang on, as Job did, to the belief that God is our hope and can carry us through.

1. Charles Spurgeon, "Fear Not," *The Spurgeon Archive* [online, cited 6 August 2013]. Available from the Internet: *spurgeon.org*.
2. L. Andrade, J. J. Caraveo-Anduaga, et al., "The Epidemiology of Major Depressive Episodes," *International Journal of Methods in Psychiatric Research 2003*, 12(3):165.
3. Adult statistic based on 6.7 percent of the adult population, as reported in "The Numbers Count: Mental Disorders in America" [online, cited 6 August 2013]. Available from the Internet: *nimh.nih.gov/health/publications*. "Nearly Two Million Teens Depressed, Government Urges Screening for All" [online], 30 March 2009 [cited 6 August 2013]. Available from the Internet: *foxnews.com*.
4. "The Numbers Count: Mental Disorders in America" [online, cited 6 August 2013]. Available from the Internet: *nimh.nih.gov/health/publications*.
5. Janice Lloyd, "CDC: Antidepressant Use Skyrockets 400% in Past 20 Years," *USA Today* [online], 20 October 2011 [cited 6 August 2013]. Available from the Internet: *usatoday30.usatoday.com*.
6. D. Martyn Lloyd-Jones, *Spiritual Depression: Its Causes and Its Cure* (Grand Rapids, MI: Eerdmans Printing Company, 1965), 18–19.
7. Edward T. Welch, *Depression: Looking Up from the Stubborn Darkness* (Greensboro, NC: New Growth Press, 2011), 28.
8. Ibid., 225–26.
9. Mike Mason, *The Gospel According to Job* (Wheaton, IL: Crossway Books, 1994), xii.

DISCONNECTION: THE FEAR OF BEING ALONE

WELCOME BACK TO THIS SMALL-GROUP DISCUSSION OF WHAT ARE YOU AFRAID OF?

The previous session's application challenge encouraged you to become more familiar with depression by reading an article, watching a movie, talking with a professional, and so on. If you're comfortable, share something interesting you learned from that experience this week.

What did you appreciate most about the study material in week 2? Why?

This session will focus on disconnection: the fear of being alone. Do you consider it a blessing or a curse when you spend a lot of time by yourself? Explain your answer.

What ideas or images come to mind when you hear the word *lonely*?

To prepare for the DVD segment, read aloud the following verses.

> *Hear, O LORD, when I cry with my voice!*
> *Have mercy also upon me, and answer me.*
> *When You said, "Seek My face,"*
> *My heart said to You, "Your face, LORD, I will seek."*
> *Do not hide Your face from me;*
> *Do not turn Your servant away in anger;*
> *You have been my help;*
> *Do not leave me nor forsake me,*
> *O God of my salvation.*
> *When my father and my mother forsake me,*
> *Then the LORD will take care of me.*
>
> PSALM 27:7-10

WATCH

COMPLETE THE VIEWER GUIDE BELOW AS YOU WATCH DVD SESSION 3.

WAYS WE BECOME DISCONNECTED

1. The disconnection of _____

_____-_____ percent of American households have just one person.

Christians who are isolated from other Christians move toward

_____.

2. The disconnection of _____

3. The disconnection of _____

WHAT WE NEED WHEN WE'RE DISCONNECTED

1. We need _____.

2. We need _____.

3. We need _____.

4. We need _____.

Life is one long experience of _____.

One day those who have refused God's offer of free grace and salvation will be disconnected from God _____.

Jesus was disconnected from God so that we could be _____ to Him.

RESPOND

*USE THE FOLLOWING QUESTIONS TO DISCUSS
THE DVD SEGMENT WITH YOUR GROUP.*

What did you appreciate most in Dr. Jeremiah's teaching?

In what ways can you empathize with Paul's situation and circumstances?

Where do you see disconnection reflected in our culture as a whole?

Where do you see disconnection reflected in the church?

What methods have you found helpful in making friends and building community?

What challenges have contributed to seasons of disconnection in your life?

Dr. Jeremiah mentioned four things we need to fight against loneliness: companionship, compassion, courage, and Christ. How can we support one another in these areas?

APPLICATION. Pray this week for opportunities to connect or reconnect with someone you care about. Be bold in taking advantage of these opportunities as they come. Be prepared to share about your experiences during the next group session.

THIS WEEK'S SCRIPTURE MEMORY. Use the memory card at the back of the book to memorize this verse:

> *The Lord is my light and my salvation;*
> *Whom shall I fear?*
> *The Lord is the strength of my life;*
> *Of whom shall I be afraid?*
>
> PSALM 27:1

ASSIGNMENT. Read week 3 and complete the activities before the next group experience. Consider going deeper into this content by reading chapter 5 in Dr. Jeremiah's book *What Are You Afraid Of?* (Tyndale, 2013).

WE ARE NOT ALONE

Here's an interesting thought: Americans today likely meet more people in a year than our great-grandparents met over the course of their lifetimes. Yet in spite of our vast number of encounters and acquaintances, most of us are far lonelier than our great-grandparents ever were.

Where's the sense in that? How can we be so connected in different communities and yet feel so disconnected in our personal lives? The answer is that there's a big difference between being *alone* and being *lonely*.

Hardly anyone is alone in today's society—not for long anyway. We're surrounded by people when we work, when we drive, and when we come home. We walk in crowds, shop in crowds, watch movies in crowds, exercise in crowds, and worship God in crowds.

But being physically close to people isn't the same as connecting with another person. Being part of a crowd doesn't ease our loneliness, for the same reason swimming in the ocean can't quench our thirst.

Paradoxically, the world today is filled with bustling crowds of isolated individuals.

As we'll see this week, both disconnection and the fear of disconnection have a negative impact on us as human beings and as followers of Christ. God said it's not good for us to be alone (see Gen. 2:18), and we can see that truth demonstrated in the lives of many individuals in God's Word.

The Bible also helps us move away from loneliness and the fear of disconnection. When we understand the danger of disconnection and realize the gift we have in our connection with Christ, we can serve as countercultural examples of the power of community in our world.

DAY 1

THE DANGER OF DISCONNECTION

During the summer of 2008, *The New York Times* writer Hal Niedzviecki decided to explore the brave new world of social media, particularly Facebook. So he set up an account and dove in. He quickly added friends—people he'd known over the years, relatives, friends of friends, and even a few tangential acquaintances here and there. He was soon astonished to discover that he had 700 online friends.

He had to admit: it was a rush! He had a new, enhanced view of his place in the world. But he wondered how Facebook friends translated into traditional friendships.

He decided to put his newfound popularity to the test. He planned a Facebook party designed to help him convert digital acquaintances into real, in-the-flesh friends. Niedzviecki invited all 700 of his connections to a local bar for a party. After looking through the various responses to his invitation, he crunched the numbers and concluded that he could reasonably expect at least 20 friends to show up.

When the day came, Niedzviecki felt excited. He showered and shaved, splashed on a little cologne, and dressed nicely, ready to put his best foot forward and meet his Facebook public. It felt like a first date. He walked into the neighborhood bar, found a seat, and waited. Then he waited some more.

After some time he greeted his first guest—a nice lady who was the friend of a friend. They made a little awkward small talk, and she finally left. Niedzviecki sat by himself until midnight, nursing his drink and wondering where everyone was.

"Seven hundred friends," he wrote, "and I was drinking alone."[1]

What qualities do you expect a true friend to possess?

How satisfied are you with your current number of genuine friends?

1	2	3	4	5	6	7	8	9	10
Unsatisfied									Satisfied

Hal Niedzviecki's experience illustrates a phenomenon spreading throughout modern society—a phenomenon that can be referred to as social isolation. As a culture, we continue inventing more and more ways to connect with other people. Yet as individuals, we feel more isolated than ever.

How have you seen social isolation reflected in modern society?

How have you seen social isolation reflected in your life?

People today feel more and more disconnected from one another and from society as a whole. Consequently, we feel more and more afraid.

MODERN DISCONNECTION

One truth we must recognize is that technology is fueling our disconnection in a big way. I'd like to focus on this subject for a moment because those who continue creating new technologies often sell them to us as antidotes for our isolation, when in reality they serve as a major cause of that isolation.

In 1998 researchers from Carnegie Mellon University studied the effects of addiction to the Internet, a new phenomenon then. They found that the more time people spent online, the more depressed and lonely they became. Robert Kraut, the lead author of the study, said people saw the Internet as a social medium, yet they derived from it only negative effects like depression and loneliness.[2]

Similar studies abounded, but few people listened. A 2008 survey found that adults were spending 30 percent of their leisuretime online. Today most Americans spend between eight and nine hours a day staring at a glowing screen—whether a computer, a TV, or a phone.[3]

But we need to ask the question, Through our preoccupation with technology, are we screening out healthy relationships?

What's your response to the previous question? Why?

I'm not labeling all electronic devices and connections as evil. Sometimes texts, social media, and other developments provide helpful links among people. They can certainly be beneficial and enjoyable in moderation.

The problem, however, is that these forms of quick communication have become the *primary* basis of our social interactions. Technology has become our default way of connecting with other human beings. As a result, it's become a major contributor to our growing sense of disconnection and our growing fear of isolation.

As members of society and especially as followers of Christ, what we need is less Facebook and more face time—and I'm not talking about the iPhone app by that name. I'm talking about old-school, face-to-face, eyeball-to-eyeball connection.

In other words, we need close relationships with real people. And there's no app for that.

In what situations or seasons of life do you typically feel lonely?

Has modern technology contributed to your feelings of loneliness or helped relieve them? Explain.

ANCIENT DISCONNECTION

I don't want to give the impression that loneliness and disconnection are purely modern problems, because they're not. People from all periods of history have experienced loneliness and disconnection for a variety of reasons, including a number of men and women whose stories are recorded in the Bible.

Think about Noah, for example. Imagine the ridicule he must have endured from the evil men around him while building the ark. Then the flood wiped out all his social connections beyond his immediate family (see Gen. 6–7). And Job, having lost his wealth, his children, and his health, had to suffer without the support of his wife (see Job 2:9).

David also experienced the pain of isolation, perhaps more than any other individual in the Old Testament. David became disconnected when King Saul, jealous of David's growing popularity, stalked him like an animal with the intent to kill him. David also experienced loneliness and betrayal during his reign as king.

> **Read the following passages of Scripture and record what they communicate about loneliness and disconnection.**
>
> **Psalm 25:16-21**
>
>
>
> **Psalm 142**

There are many other biblical characters we could discuss. But I'd like to spend the majority of this week focusing on the apostle Paul as our vehicle for exploring loneliness and disconnection on a deeper level.

If that sounds a little strange to you, I understand. The Bible makes it abundantly clear that Paul was an energetic, charge-ahead, type-A, goal-oriented man—a thoroughgoing people person. So how could Paul have ever experienced loneliness and isolation?

The answer is that Paul had no choice. Near the end of his life, he was arrested by Roman authorities and confined to the infamous Mamertine Prison in the bowels of Rome. From that depressing location Paul wrote the final letter of his apostolic ministry—the letter we know as 2 Timothy.

> **When have the actions of others pushed you toward disconnection and loneliness?**

Over the next couple of days we'll explore 2 Timothy to gain an understanding of Paul's experiences with disconnection. Because if anyone would be easy prey for loneliness, it would be a gregarious people person like Paul.

Paul was also the right person to provide a spiritual answer for disconnection and the fear of loneliness—an answer we can still apply to our lives today.

DAY 2

THE PAIN OF ISOLATION

Most of us don't realize how insidious true isolation can be. Going without food or water kills the body, but a lack of relationships kills the mind and the spirit. If you think I'm exaggerating, read these words from an article in *Psychology Today:*

> There is no more destructive influence on physical and mental health than the isolation of you from me and of us from them. [Isolation] has been shown to be a central agent in the etiology [cause, origin] of depression, paranoia, schizophrenia, rape, suicide, mass murder, and a wide variety of disease states.[4]

What's your initial reaction to the previous paragraph?

The simple truth is that something inside us—some key part of our core essence as human beings—doesn't like too much solitude. As God said at the beginning of human history, "It is not good that man should be alone" (Gen. 2:18). This assessment goes beyond marriage, of course. God created us to function in many types of relationships.

What emotions do you experience when you're alone?

How do you typically seek connections with other people?

Isolation and disconnection hurt us so severely because we were created with a built-in desire for social interaction. To put it simply, we need one another. None of us can live sanely without some form of regular social interaction.

That's why it's helpful for us to learn from Paul's experiences with disconnection.

THE REALITY OF ISOLATION

We don't know many details of Paul's final stay in the Roman prison, but we know the situation was bleak. For one thing, the physical conditions of Paul's imprisonment were terrible, according to scholar John Phillips:

> In Paul's day, the name of that dungeon was spoken in whispers. It was a black pit, a hole in the ground. It was damp and chilly. The bed was a clump of stale, damp straw, and the floor was heaped with filth. There was a spring, at least, but the air was foul. Food was lowered to prisoners from time to time—rough fare to keep body and soul together—and perhaps a kidskin of thin, sour wine.[5]

What kinds of physical locations or atmospheres make you feel lonely? Why?

Furthermore, Paul was more than a little unsettled and uncertain about his future. He faced a trial before the Roman emperor Nero, a brutal man with a known hatred for Christians. Paul understood that he had only a small chance of escaping with his life:

I am already being poured out as a drink offering, and the time of my departure is at hand.
2 TIMOTHY 4:6

How does the awareness of death and mortality contribute to our feelings of loneliness?

Perhaps worst of all, Paul was forced to endure physical discomfort and the knowledge of his imminent death without support or encouragement from his friends. He was disconnected from the people he cared about because they had abandoned him in his time of need, his first trial in Rome:

At my first defense no one stood with me, but all forsook me. May it not be charged against them.
2 TIMOTHY 4:16

When have you felt abandoned or unsupported by the people you care about most?

How often do you feel frightened by the possibility that your friends and family won't be there when you need them?

1	2	3	4	5	6	7	8	9	10
Rarely									Daily

The reality is that most of us will never experience the kind of forced isolation Paul went through in prison. Even if we committed a crime and were placed in a modern jail, we'd still have opportunities to connect with others and the outside world.

But we don't have to be in a cold, wet place to feel alone. In truth there are lonely office cubicles all over the world. There are church pews loaded with friendless individuals every week. There are sky-high condominiums with people packed tightly together, yet although they encounter one another every day, they never learn one another's names.

Many people also become trapped in prisons built by circumstances. For example, divorce is a grinding factory for loneliness. Victims of divorce lose not only their mates but also many of their friends. Some friends choose a side; others back away from both parties. One woman told me that she had never felt so alone as in the days that followed the end of her marriage.

Our modern world has also seen a sharp increase in the number of people living alone. In 1950 9 percent of American households were the home to just one person.[6] By 2012 that figure escalated to 28 percent.[7]

What has most recently caused you to feel the pain of isolation?

How were you supported or uplifted in the midst of that pain?

THE NEED FOR RELATIONSHIPS

I believe we can explain something of our growing disconnection from others by comparing it to a primary principle of physics. The second law of thermodynamics, also known as the law of entropy, states that life, energy, and matter are always moving toward disorder and disorganization. Things break down; centers don't hold. Entropy happens in all systems.

We see evidence for this concept all the time even if we don't make a connection with the law of entropy. For example, if you leave a piece of fruit on your kitchen counter for a week, what happens? Does it remain in a continued state of freshness or continue growing until you're ready to eat it? No, the fruit disintegrates from the inside out. It breaks down and rots.

The same principle is true for buildings left uninhabited, gardens left untended, stars burning in the void of space, and physical bodies. Everything that physically exists in the universe right now is on a journey toward its ultimate destruction.

Summarize the law of entropy in your own words.

What are some ways we try to fight against the law of entropy in modern society?

The second law of thermodynamics applies to objects that have physical mass, but the principle can apply to social systems as well—human relationships, societies, and civilizations. All of these can break down if they're not maintained. The difference between the way social systems and physical entities respond to the law of entropy is that the breakdown of social systems is preventable. Relationships and other social systems will break down if we allow them to, but such entropy can be resisted. And it's my opinion that we must resist relational entropy if our society is going to survive.

Where do you see evidence of entropy in our culture's relationships and social systems?

When people come together and form communities, they enrich one another simply by virtue of their different gifts and personalities. When we work together, we're greater than the sum of our parts. That's what Solomon wanted to teach in this famous Scripture passage:

> *Two are better than one,*
> *Because they have a good reward for their labor.*
> *For if they fall, one will lift up his companion.*
> *But woe to him who is alone when he falls,*
> *For he has no one to help him up.*
> *Again, if two lie down together, they will keep warm;*
> *But how can one be warm alone?*
> *Though one may be overpowered by another,*
> *   two can withstand him.*
> *And a threefold cord is not quickly broken.*
> ECCLESIASTES 4:9-12

People in relationships have a better chance of resisting entropy—thus keeping culture ordered and organized—than those who are isolated. Broken marriages send shock waves through society and hurt us all by increasing the tendency toward disintegration. Churches that experience conflict and break apart hurt God's kingdom, as well as their communities, by fracturing relational bonds and destroying unity. Revolving-door workplaces harm society because they undermine permanence and foster chaos.

How have you been blessed and encouraged by long-term relationships in your life?

Long-lasting relationships are the unifying force that creates accountable, healthy social stability. As followers of Christ, we must build these relationships in order to erect a bulwark against disconnection and the fear of isolation.

DAY 3

THE PAIN OF ABANDONMENT

Many things in this world are unreliable—machines, businesses, and governments, for example. Yet maddeningly, we're sometimes forced to rely on the very things we know to be unreliable.

Airlines are a good example of this phenomenon. When we plan a vacation or purchase a flight for a business trip, we're placing a great deal of faith in an airline to have our plane ready and waiting when we're scheduled to leave. At the same time, we know that numerous factors can cause delays or even cancellations for thousands of flights each day, so we have no real guarantee that our trip will proceed as scheduled.

> **When have you recently been forced to rely on something you knew was unreliable?**

> **What are some ways you try to protect yourself against the unreliability of machines and systems?**

We've learned this week that God created you and me to function best when we're invested in relationships with other people; it's not good for us to be alone. We've also learned that long-term relationships help us weather the storms of life and can even add stability to our society as a whole.

In other words, we've been created to rely on other people. But unfortunately, because many people are unreliable, establishing relationships can be a risky business. As we'll see from 2 Timothy, Paul understood this truth from experience.

> **Do you consider yourself to be a reliable person? Explain.**

THE DISCONNECTION OF DESERTION

At some point during his missionary journeys, Paul encountered and befriended a man named Demas. We don't know much about Demas personally, but we know that he participated in Paul's ministry for an extended period of time. Indeed, Paul mentioned Demas by name in two of the New Testament letters he wrote during his first stay in a Roman prison (see Col. 4:14; Philem. 24).

Demas's name came up again in Paul's second letter to Timothy, but something had changed. Despite his earlier willingness to minister with Paul and spread the good news, Demas eventually proved to be unreliable:

> *Be diligent to come to me quickly; for Demas has forsaken me, having loved this present world, and has departed for Thessalonica—Crescens for Galatia, Titus for Dalmatia.*
> 2 TIMOTHY 4:9-10

We don't know all the details, but apparently, Demas was again in Rome when Paul was sentenced and thrown into jail for a second time. This time, however, the situation was much more intense. Christians were being persecuted throughout the Roman Empire with the blessing of Nero, the emperor.

Notice Paul's use of strong words in the previous verses. He noted that Demas had "forsaken" him because he "loved this present world" (v. 10). Some scholars speculate that the Romans had turned up the heat on the Christian community in Rome itself, resulting in Paul's imprisonment. These scholars suggest that Demas didn't want to end up in a dungeon like his friend, so he ran.

What ideas or images come to mind when you hear the word *forsaken?* **Why?**

Demas wasn't the only one of Paul's ministry partners to leave when the going got tough. Here's what Paul wrote at the beginning of his epistle:

> *This you know, that all those in Asia have turned away from me, among whom are Phygellus and Hermogenes.*
> 2 TIMOTHY 1:15

Similarly, Paul was left alone and unsupported during the first trial after his arrest:

> *At my first defense no one stood with me, but all forsook me. May it not be charged against them.*
> 2 TIMOTHY 4:16

No one but faithful Luke (see v. 11) stayed behind to keep Paul company and help him endure the long days of waiting while the Roman bureaucratic processes took their ponderous course. Paul had been almost completely abandoned, and he was forced to contemplate that abandonment alone in his dungeon cell.

How have you tried to protect yourself against the unreliability of other people?

How have your efforts to protect yourself contributed to your experiences with loneliness or the fear of loneliness?

THE DISCONNECTION OF INTERFERENCE

In addition to being abandoned by some people he cared about, Paul also experienced disconnection when someone actively worked against him:

> *Alexander the coppersmith did me much harm. May the Lord repay him according to his works. You also must beware of him, for he has greatly resisted our words.*
> 2 TIMOTHY 4:14-15

That phrase "did me much harm" (v. 14) literally means "informed many evil things against me." For that reason some scholars speculate that Alexander was a Judas figure who betrayed Paul to Roman authorities, resulting in his imprisonment. That makes sense in light of Paul's warning to Timothy: "You also must beware of him" (v. 15).

Regardless of the details, Alexander was a man who resisted Paul's ministry—who interfered in Paul's work of advancing the gospel. Sadly, this is a common experience for those who choose to follow Christ.

How have you experienced resistance or interference in your efforts to live as a follower of Christ?

As Christians, we need to understand that there will always be people who resist us and attempt to disrupt what we try to accomplish. If we're doing what God calls us to do, we'll always experience interference in one form or another.

Indeed, the greater our commitment to Christ, the more we'll be disconnected from the values of the crowd. Disconnection from the culture's pervasive values often breeds resentment, and resentment breeds opposition. In other words, those in the world often don't appreciate our efforts to help them.

As Jesus said:

> *If you were of the world, the world would love its own. Yet because you are not of the world, but I chose you out of the world, therefore the world hates you.*
> JOHN 15:19

How have you experienced hatred from the world?

Sadly, fellow Christians can also push us toward disconnection. Those who lack our commitment often desert us or disappoint us as they retreat into society's less demanding values, finding comfort in numbers. Sometimes these are people into whom we've poured our lives, and we're devastated. That's what happened to Paul.

If this happens to us, we need to remember that it's simply part of our calling to discipleship. We can't worry about what others do; we can only focus on not becoming deserters or interferers ourselves. And instead of allowing such an incident to create disconnection in our lives, we can seek the fellowship of our Father and our Christian friends to find the loving support we need.

DAY 4

FEAR PROFILE: JOSEPH

This week we're exploring disconnection and isolation, along with the fear they often produce in our lives. As human beings, we've been created for community. We intuitively know it's not good for us to be alone—not for long periods of time anyway—so we're terrified by the thought of being abandoned or betrayed by those we care about.

Most of us experience true isolation in short bursts. We have temporary seasons in life when we feel deeply alone and disconnected from our loved ones—even disconnected from our culture. Perhaps we move to a new city, for example, or we contract an illness that removes us from our social patterns for a time. But most of us have the ability to form new relationships or reenter a relational routine.

Even so, short encounters with true isolation are acutely painful on a number of levels. They affect us emotionally, mentally, spiritually, and even physically. In other words, even brief encounters with genuine loneliness can produce enough fear to greatly affect our lives and relationships.

> When have you experienced times of genuine loneliness?

> To what degree are you currently affected or motivated by the fear of loneliness?
>
> | 1 | 2 | 3 | 4 | 5 | 6 | 7 | 8 | 9 | 10 |
> |---|---|---|---|---|---|---|---|---|----|
> A minor degree   A major degree

Today I want to continue our exploration of disconnection and the fear of loneliness by focusing on the Old Testament character Joseph. We know Joseph best because of his intriguing story. This young Hebrew man was betrayed by his family and sold into slavery. Nevertheless, he became one of the most powerful men of his day.

It's a great story. But as we'll see, Joseph's life was also marked by a variety of profound experiences with disconnection.

DISCONNECTED AT BIRTH

When we look back at Joseph's family history, it's clear that he experienced a high level of disconnection even from his earliest days. Joseph's father, Jacob (also called Israel), had two wives and two concubines: Rachel, Leah, Bilhah, and Zilpah. Rachel was the only woman in that group whom Jacob truly loved, yet for years she was also the only woman who didn't bear children—until Joseph arrived.

Jacob quickly made it clear that Joseph, the son of the woman he loved, was now his favorite child. He treated Joseph differently from his other sons, even to the point of giving Joseph extravagant gifts.

As you might expect, such behavior didn't endear Joseph to the rest of his siblings:

> *Israel loved Joseph more than all his children, because he was the son of his old age. Also he made him a tunic of many colors. But when his brothers saw that their father loved him more than all his brothers, they hated him and could not speak peaceably to him.*
> GENESIS 37:3-4

It didn't help matters that Joseph was a bit spoiled. He lorded his preferential treatment over his brothers and even told them about a series of dreams that indicated they would one day bow down before him (see vv. 5-11).

What are some character flaws that often cause people to disconnect or distance themselves from others?

How have you contributed to your own experiences with loneliness?

In the course of time, Joseph's brothers followed their hatred down a dark road. When Joseph was sent to check on them in the middle of the wilderness, they captured him, beat him, and threw him into an empty cistern.

The brothers' original plan was to murder Joseph in cold blood, but instead they sold him as a slave to a band of traders on their way to Egypt. Using their brother's bloody tunic as evidence, they convinced their father that Joseph had been devoured by a wild animal. Then they went on with their lives, glad to be rid of him (see vv. 12-36).

The upshot was that Joseph experienced an entirely new form of disconnection and isolation. Whereas he had previously been emotionally and affectionately detached from most of his family, he was now physically isolated from everything he'd ever known. He was also culturally cut off from those around him, having been swept into a new country, a new social class, and a new way of life in a matter of hours.

What events have caused the most radical changes in your life?

Joseph was ultimately sold to a man named Potiphar, and although his life couldn't be described as glamorous by any stretch of the imagination, his situation improved. Potiphar recognized Joseph as a hard worker and an honest man, eventually promoting him as the overseer of the entire household.

Unfortunately, just as Alexander's interference contributed to Paul's disconnection, Joseph was also the victim of slander and abuse. To make a long story short, Potiphar's wife was attracted to Joseph and wanted to sleep with him. When he refused, she framed him for attempted rape (see Gen. 39:1-20).

The result was that Joseph once again found himself dislodged from everything he'd known. His isolation and loneliness must have intensified as even his freedom was taken away.

How often do you think about the possibility that other people might be planning to harm you or betray you?

1	2	3	4	5	6	7	8	9	10
Rarely									Daily

What do you dislike most about being abused or slandered by others? Why?

Just as in Potiphar's house, Joseph made the most of his situation in prison. He was eventually placed in a position of authority over the other prisoners, and unlike his early behavior with his brothers, he used his authority for the benefit of the people around him (see vv. 21-23).

Joseph even went out of his way to assist a fellow prisoner who'd been the chief butler for Pharaoh. When the butler was returned to his post, however, he forgot about Joseph's kindness. Joseph was abandoned once again.

> **Read Genesis 40. How did this situation contribute to Joseph's sense of disconnection and isolation?**

Joseph spent more than 13 years in slavery and imprisonment. He was disconnected from the people he loved most. He was forced to adjust over and over again to new people, new places, and new forms of humiliation.

So how did he endure it all? How did he fight against the disconnection and loneliness inherent in his circumstances? Let's find out.

> **What methods do you typically use to combat loneliness and the fear of disconnection?**

CONNECTED TO GOD

Joseph was able to survive his experiences with disconnection because he committed to maintain a strong connection with God and because God was faithful to bless His servant. For example, here's what Scripture says about Joseph's early experiences in Potiphar's house:

> *The Lord was with Joseph, and he was a successful man; and he was in the house of his master the Egyptian. And his master saw that the Lord was with him and that the Lord made all he did to prosper in his hand.*
> **GENESIS 39:2-3**

Don't miss the point of these verses. It wasn't important in the grand scheme of things that Joseph was successful in Potiphar's house or that he was promoted. Rather, the vital element in those verses is that first phrase: "The LORD was with Joseph" (v. 2).

Even in the depths of his isolation, Joseph wasn't alone. When he was disconnected from everyone and everything he once knew, he still had God. Just as importantly, Joseph reached out to God and embraced His presence rather than succumbing to loneliness and the fears that come with it.

In other words, Joseph fought his disconnection from the world by clinging to his connection with God, not just once but multiple times throughout his ordeals in Egypt.

How would you assess your relationship with and awareness of God in recent weeks?

1	2	3	4	5	6	7	8	9	10

Disconnected   Connected

How do you typically try to connect with God?

What are some new methods you can use to seek God's presence in the midst of disconnection?

Thankfully, Joseph's story didn't end in prison. When Pharaoh needed help interpreting a pair of prophetic dreams, the chief butler finally remembered Joseph, who was summoned to interpret the dreams. Joseph then became the second most powerful man in Egypt and used his authority to save thousands of people from starvation during a terrible famine, including his family (see Gen. 41–42:6). So not only was God faithful to Joseph during his many trials, but His plan also allowed Joseph to rescue his people during their time of need.

Through it all Joseph wasn't destroyed by disconnection and loneliness, because he intentionally focused on his connection with God. As we'll see tomorrow, the same can be true for us.

DAY 5

HOW TO WIN AGAINST DISCONNECTION

You may have noticed that I use a lot of strong words when it comes to the different ways we can respond to our fears and to the causes of those fears. For example, I've talked about *facing* the fear of failure and *combating* experiences with depression. I've encouraged you to *fight* against loneliness and the fear of being alone.

These word choices are intentional, because the worst thing we can do in the face of our fears is to be passive. We must be active in confronting fear. We must be intentional if we want to break free from our fears and live as God intends for us to live.

What obstacles prevent you from actively fighting your fears?

What actions have helped you address those obstacles in the past?

Let's finish this week's study by refocusing on Paul's methods for fighting against the disconnection and isolation he experienced near the end of his life. Specifically, let's look at four action steps we can take when we face disconnection in our lives.

1. FIND COMPANIONSHIP

Take a moment to remember Paul's situation. He was almost certainly alone in the dank Mamertine Prison in Rome, the last stop on the road to death for the empire's most feared prisoners. The church in Rome had abandoned him, probably because its members were lying low to avoid Paul's fate.

Given everything Paul experienced in that prison, his final words to Timothy should come as no surprise:

> *Be diligent to come to me quickly. Get Mark and bring him with you, for he is useful to me for ministry. Do your utmost to come before winter.*
> 2 TIMOTHY 4:9,11,21

Paul had been betrayed. He'd been abandoned. He was lonely. For all those reasons Paul asked Timothy to help by coming to see him. He knew he needed companionship, so he asked for it.

Do you feel comfortable asking your friends and family members to spend time with you? Explain.

Let's get something clear. If the apostle Paul—perhaps the strongest and most mature Christian in history—longed and pleaded for companionship in his final days, how much more should we acknowledge our own need for companions? How much more should we plead for help to combat our disconnection and loneliness?

And I should clarify that we need companionship from our friends in the flesh, not just friends in pixels and digital sound bites. I'm talking about friends who can wipe our tears and hug our necks and squeeze our hands as they earnestly pray with us.

Of course, that assumes we have such friends. One of the greatest omissions in the life of the average American Christian is the failure to cultivate close companions in the faith. Simply attending Sunday-morning worship isn't enough to create those connections. Many churches have implemented small-group ministries to foster the kinds of relationships needed to "stir up love and good works" (Heb. 10:24).

The reality is that every Christian needs to have close companions in the faith, whether through small groups or other means. Finding ourselves alone in the middle of a crisis isn't a good time to realize we have no one we can turn to.

Action step 1: Make a point to have deep interaction with a close friend or family member this week.

2. FIND COMPASSION

Paul's last words to Timothy include a request that seems a bit out of place in the pages of Scripture:

> *Bring the cloak that I left with Carpus at Troas when you come— and the books, especially the parchments.*
> 2 TIMOTHY 4:13

Actually, Paul's words make perfect sense in the context of a letter to his friend. Indeed, his request highlights our universal need for kindness and compassion. Paul was cold in his dungeon cell. He was bored, and he asked his friend for help. And that really is OK.

How does it make you feel to help others in need? Why?

One reason we fear disconnection is that when our deepest needs rise to the surface, we worry we'll have no one to meet those needs—no one to help us. At the same time, we live in a culture that praises rugged individualism, which makes us feel that we should be able to handle everything ourselves. We're constantly living in the tension between our need for help and our desire to appear that we've got everything under control. That's stressful.

What emotions do you experience when you ask for help? Why?

Where do you turn for compassionate help?

When we desperately need something, we shouldn't hesitate to ask our loyal friends for it. That kind of honesty is a great way to fight against disconnection and the fear of loneliness.

Action step 2: Allow a friend to demonstrate kindness by asking him or her for a favor this week.

3. FIND COURAGE

All of us understand that isolation and loneliness can be scary. We also know that the antidote to fear is courage. But what builds courage? How do we gain or grow courage as followers of Christ?

Courage doesn't come from willpower or a pep rally or the power of positive thinking. Instead, true courage comes through faith in God.

What ideas or images come to mind when you hear the word *courage?* Why?

All of us have a choice. Either we look at the future in fear of what might happen, or we look at the future with faith directed toward our sovereign Father and God—the One who holds all things in His hands. Faith leads to trust in God, and trust in God leads us to act according to His will even in the face of fear. That's courage.

In prison Paul found courage by demonstrating his faith in God's Word:

> *Bring the cloak that I left with Carpus at Troas when you come—* ***and the books, especially the parchments.***
>
> 2 TIMOTHY 4:13, EMPHASIS ADDED

Books and *parchments* may have referred to the Scriptures of the Old Testament or to a collection of Jesus' teachings. When things got tough, Paul turned to the Scriptures to find courage and strength. What a blessing that we can do the same—and that we don't have to wait for a special delivery in order to access God's Word.

Action step 3: Demonstrate your faith in God's Word this week by memorizing 2 Timothy 1:7.

4. FIND CHRIST

Just as Joseph turned to God during a time of extreme disconnection, Paul's words to Timothy remind us that we're never truly alone when we know Christ. God has promised never to leave us or forsake us (see Heb. 13:5), and we demonstrate faith when we hang on to that truth even when we don't feel His presence. Remember: it's not what we feel that counts; it's what we know:

> *At my first defense no one stood with me, but all forsook me. May it not be charged against them. But the Lord stood with me and strengthened me, so that the message might be preached fully through me, and that all the Gentiles might hear. Also I was delivered out of the mouth of the lion. And the Lord will deliver me from every evil work and preserve me for His heavenly kingdom. To Him be glory forever and ever. Amen!*
>
> 2 TIMOTHY 4:16-18

What's your initial reaction to the previous verses?

Being disconnected from other people isn't good. But when it happens, God can use the situation to help us make the transition from enjoying the *physical* presence of others to experiencing the *spiritual* presence of Himself. This reveals an essential difference between our earthly parents and our heavenly one: mothers and fathers know they must someday let go; they can't be with us forever. Not so with God. Once we come to know Him, we can live with the assurance that we'll never be separated from Him.

How do you typically take advantage of your opportunities to connect with Christ?

Action step 4: Set aside at least an hour this week to spend solely in God's presence.

God doesn't want us to be alone. He's done everything possible to ensure that we can live connected lives in harmonious human relationships. But those relationships merely foreshadow our eternal relationship with God Himself.

The question, then, is this: Are you confident that Christ is always with you and that you'll always be with Christ? Placing your faith in Him is the only way to be sure that you'll never be alone again.

1. Hal Niedzviecki, "Facebook in a Crowd," *The New York Times Magazine* [online], 24 October 2008 [cited 20 August 2013]. Available from the Internet: *nytimes.com*.
2. Jerry Adler, "Online and Bummed Out: One Study Says the Internet Can Be Alienating," *Newsweek* 132, no. 37 (14 September 1998): 84.
3. Nicholas Carr, *The Shallows: What the Internet Is Doing to Our Brains* (New York: W. W. Norton, 2011), 86–87.
4. Philip Zimbardo, "The Age of Indifference," *Psychology Today,* 30 August 1980, as quoted by Charles R. Swindoll, *The Tale of the Tardy Oxcart and 1,501 Other Stories* (Nashville: Thomas Nelson, 1998).
5. John Phillips, *Exploring the Pastoral Epistles,* The John Phillips Commentary Series (Grand Rapids, MI: Kregel Publications, 2004), 449–50.
6. Bobby Allyn, "More Singles Living Alone and Loving It, Despite the Economy," *USA Today* [online], 27 April 2012 [cited 20 August 2013]. Available from the Internet: *usatoday30.usatoday.com*.
7. James Joyner, "Record 28 Percent of American Households One Person Only," *Outside the Beltway* [online], 1 February 2012 [cited 20 August 2013]. Available from the Internet: *outsidethebeltway.com*.

DISEASE: THE FEAR OF SERIOUS ILLNESS

WELCOME BACK TO THIS SMALL-GROUP DISCUSSION OF WHAT ARE YOU AFRAID OF?

The previous session's application challenge involved connecting or reconnecting with someone you care about. If you're comfortable, talk about the emotions you experienced before and after connecting with that person.

What did you appreciate most about the study material in week 3? Why?

If you could write a message from the church to people who are suffering from loneliness, what would you say?

This session will focus on disease: the fear of serious illness. What words describe your experiences with illness during your lifetime? Why?

To prepare for the DVD segment, read aloud the following verses.

> *In those days Hezekiah was sick and near death. And Isaiah the prophet, the son of Amoz, went to him and said to him, "Thus says the LORD: 'Set your house in order, for you shall die and not live.' " Then Hezekiah turned his face toward the wall, and prayed to the LORD, and said, "Remember now, O LORD, I pray, how I have walked before You in truth and with a loyal heart, and have done what is good in Your sight." And Hezekiah wept bitterly.*
> ISAIAH 38:1-3

WATCH

PROBABLE ENCOUNTERS WITH DISEASE

When Adam and Eve sinned, _____ became a grim reality. Death became unavoidable.

Disease: any condition that causes _____, dysfunction, distress, social problems, or _____

PRIMARY EXAMPLES OF DISEASE

Paul	Job	Lazarus	The woman with the issue of blood
Naaman	David	Asa	Jehoram People of Galilee
Epaphroditus		Dorcas	

PAINFUL EMOTIONS OF DISEASE

1. The _____

   _____ and _____—that's always an understandable
   response to disease.

2. The _____

   Medicine and doctors have a part in _____.

3. The _____

   God's perfect will for us may not exempt us from illness, but He knows how to turn
   all things for what's _____ for us.

PRACTICAL ENCOURAGEMENTS OF DISEASE

1. Control your _____.

   Don't let temporal illness steal your eternal _____.

2. Count your _____.

   The Lord can teach us many lessons in _____ that could never
   be learned in _____.

3. Continue your _____.

   Going through a rough patch often equips us for further _____, and
   sometimes it allows us to empathize and minister to people who otherwise would
   never have crossed our paths or been touched by our lives.

RESPOND

*USE THE FOLLOWING QUESTIONS TO DISCUSS
THE DVD SEGMENT WITH YOUR GROUP.*

What did you appreciate most in Dr. Jeremiah's teaching?

What do you dislike most about being sick? Why?

Respond to Dr. Jeremiah's statements: "There are things far worse than disease. God's perfect will for us may not exempt us from illness, but He knows how to turn all things for what's best for us."

Do you find it easy or difficult to control your mind and rein in your thoughts when you face difficult circumstances? Explain.

What are some of the main blessings in your life now?

What steps can you take to be more mindful of those blessings in the face of illness and other challenges?

How would you define or summarize the work God has assigned you to do in this season of life?

APPLICATION. Before concluding this group session, record any prayer requests from group members in connection with disease. Commit to pray for the members of your group every day for the next week.

THIS WEEK'S SCRIPTURE MEMORY. Use the memory card at the back of the book to memorize this verse:

> *God has not given us a spirit of fear, but of power and of love and of a sound mind.*
> 2 TIMOTHY 1:7

ASSIGNMENT. Read week 4 and complete the activities before the next group experience. Consider going deeper into this content by reading chapter 2 in Dr. Jeremiah's book *What Are You Afraid Of?* (Tyndale, 2013).

BODY BREAKDOWN

Every year it seems as if a new disease with an exotic name comes out of the woodwork, makes a splash in the news, and scares millions—all while afflicting only a relatively small number of people. Do you remember SARS, for example? Mad-cow disease? The dreaded West-Nile virus? What about the bird flu or the H1N1 virus (also known as the swine flu) in recent years?

These days I pay much more attention to the commonplace illnesses that regularly afflict me and the members of my congregation—the ones that have been assaulting humanity for thousands of years. I'm talking about cancer. Heart disease. Alzheimer's. Stroke. Diabetes. Parkinson's.

For me and the members of my generation, along with millions of others around the world, these diseases are the true bogeymen of modern life. The specter of these and other illnesses is what keeps us up at night and causes us to feel afraid.

The truth is, we all fear disease. Even when we're young and feel indestructible, we still know in the back of our minds that our bodies are fragile. We still feel the threat of breakdown when viruses, bacteria, or injuries drain some of the energy and physical strength we've always known.

Maybe you're battling an illness right now. Maybe you're facing one just around the next corner, or perhaps someone dear to you is desperately fighting for his or her health. The reality is that one or more diseases will eventually catch up with each of us. And for most of us, illness will be the vehicle by which we transition to eternity—a thought that can be frightening, even for those of us who know where we're headed.

Disease is prevalent and inevitable, but it doesn't have to control us or drive us into panic or despair. The way we understand disease and its effect on us makes a great difference in our ability to cope with it. Thankfully, the Bible has much to say about disease and our natural fear of illness. It even offers practical advice for facing that fear while remaining productive citizens of God's kingdom.

DAY 1

THE PREVALENCE OF DISEASE

In recent decades scientists have become expertly efficient at identifying and cataloging many viruses, bacteria, contagions, and other causes of sickness in the human body. As a result, medical libraries around the world are filled with information about such sicknesses, including causes, symptoms, and sometimes cures.

Because of my personal experiences in recent years, however, the concept of disease has become condensed into a single word that is both profoundly personal and ultimately unsettling. That word is *cancer*.

> **What ideas or experiences come to mind when you hear the word** *cancer*? **Why?**

> **How would you summarize your recent experiences with sickness?**

I was first diagnosed with non-Hodgkin's lymphoma in 1994. That was when I met with my oncologist and his team of doctors, all of whom worked together to save my life. Now don't misunderstand me; I know God holds my life in His hands, and I give Him the glory for my recovery. But I also understand that God raises up caring, gifted people to apply their skills as His agents in delivering His gift of health. I'm so grateful for these talented specialists, and I let them know it in every way I can.

To be frank, cancer is one of those subjects that can't be comprehended secondhand. It's larger than life, and a positive diagnosis carries such powerful implications that it changes a person forever. So I won't recall the details of my bout with cancer here, and I sincerely hope you never have to experience that fight.

What I can talk about is the fear and helplessness that come with the diagnosis of any serious disease. That's something I think we can all understand or imagine.

Because I'm a pastor, people are often curious about my reaction to being diagnosed with a potentially fatal illness. The question they almost always ask is some variation of "Were you afraid?"

Here's how I answered that question in my book *When Your World Falls Apart*:

> Absolutely! I was *desperately* afraid. There's no disputing that. Was I afraid to die? No. I'm not afraid to leave this life, although I'm not eager to do so either. A good bit of my fear focused on losing precious years with the people I love. Some of it was simply about pain. Some of it was about the unknown. How would you respond to the news that you were suffering from a possibly fatal disease? Imagine the thoughts and feelings that might flood your heart at such a time, and you'll know the same things I experienced.[1]

What's your response to the previous sentiments?

What I've come to understand and what I hope to communicate this week is that Christ can overcome every fear we face. That's a message that can change the world, and it's certainly a vital truth that can change your life.

SICKNESS IS PERVASIVE

One reason diseases are so distasteful and disruptive is that they affect so many areas of our lives. Sickness starts on a physical level, of course, but it doesn't end there.

What's the most physically sick you've ever been?

How have you experienced turmoil and disruption because of physical illness?

Serious diseases take an emotional toll as well. Negative emotions such as fear, doubt, and confusion quickly drain us of emotional energy. We get tired of feeling sick, tired of being tired, and tired of wishing we could just get better already!

It's also becoming increasingly common for diseases to affect people financially. In fact, the United States is the most expensive nation for treating illness.[2] Amazingly, in 2010 the total cost for health care in the United States was more than $2.5 trillion.[3]

Because of these astronomical costs, a major medical incident can wipe out a family that's living on the financial edge. Often, when our bodily health declines, so does the health of our bank accounts.

> **Where have you seen sickness and disease linked with financial distress in today's culture?**

> **What other areas of life are affected when we're forced to deal with a serious disease?**

The word *disease* (dis-ease) literally carries the idea of being *not easy* or *not at ease,* and our experiences confirm the accuracy of that meaning. Disease disrupts the ordinary patterns of life, robbing us of control and forming barriers with other people. It sends us to expensive medical facilities, where we place our lives in the hands of strangers. It builds our reliance on mystifying medications. It pushes us toward isolation, loneliness, and depression.

Of course, all this discomfort makes sense when we remember that disease wasn't part of God's original plan for our lives. We weren't meant to deal with illness at all.

SICKNESS IS OUT OF PLACE

It's hard for us to imagine anyone living in perfect health, but that's what Adam and Eve experienced. Their bodies were absolutely flawless. The very concept of disease would have been foreign to them, as would the idea of working out to maintain their physical health. Alas, such perfection didn't last.

Sin shattered that reality. It cost Adam and Eve (and us) God's gift of paradise, and it corrupted the whole created order. As Paul told us, God's creation (including people) is now afflicted with disease and corruption, and as a result, it groans in agony:

We know that the whole creation groans and labors with birth pangs together until now. Not only that, but we also who have the firstfruits of the Spirit, even we ourselves groan within ourselves, eagerly waiting for the adoption, the redemption of our body.

ROMANS 8:22-23

Because of Adam and Eve's rebellion, disease is now a prevalent part of our existence. Each of us will spend a certain portion of our lives sick, wounded, or dying.

Yet even in the midst of our illnesses, we understand on a basic level that it wasn't supposed to be this way. We weren't designed to deal with sickness and disease—not originally. Therefore, each instance of illness only makes us more aware of the way sin has corrupted us to the core.

Read the following verses and record what they teach about God's original design for humanity.

Genesis 1:26-27

Ecclesiastes 3:11

In short, we feel that sickness is an intrusion into our physical selves because that's exactly the case. We were created as eternal beings, but instead, we're forced to settle for the corruption of everything we hold dear.

It's no wonder we wait "eagerly," as Paul said in Romans 8:23, for the redemption of our bodies. But as we'll see tomorrow, that kind of waiting can really be hard.

DAY 2

THE PAIN OF DISEASE

I've never preached a sermon series on "Diseased Characters in the Bible," nor has any pastor I know. But I'll admit that's an interesting idea, and there would certainly be a wealth of material to mine. Like our world today, the Bible is filled with men and women who experienced physical illness.

Consider the following.

- Job sitting on his ash heap, covered with boils (see Job 2:7-8)
- Lazarus, a man with a terminal illness (see John 11:1)
- The woman with the issue of blood (see Mark 5:25)
- Naaman and his leprosy (see 2 Kings 5:1)
- King Asa and his foot disease (see 1 Kings 15:23)
- King Jehoram and his diseased intestines (see 2 Chron. 21:15)
- Epaphroditus, who was "sick almost unto death" (Phil. 2:27; see vv. 25-27)
- Dorcas, who got sick, died, and was raised from death by Peter (see Acts 9:36-41)

One of the things I appreciate most about Scripture is the way it captures real people in real situations. Therefore, when it describes people who are sick and desperate, they typically demonstrate the kinds of emotions you'd expect a sick and desperate person to feel. Conversely, when the Bible tells the story of someone who experienced healing from illness, we often get a clear picture of the joy they felt.

> **Read the following passages of Scripture and record the different emotions and reactions presented.**
>
> Psalm 41:4-12
>
>
> Luke 17:11-19
>
>
> John 11:17-37

What fears and other emotions do you typically experience when you're sick?

What fears and other emotions do you experience when you're around others who are sick?

The story of Hezekiah in the Old Testament gives us an honest, full-bodied look at the emotional ups and downs that accompany any struggle with disease. We'll explore his story over the next couple of days.

A SUCCESSFUL LIFE

Hezekiah was a descendant of David and a king of Judah, and if that makes you assume he was a bad guy, I understand. Many of the Old Testament kings were despicable human beings for one reason or another.

But Hezekiah wasn't an evil king. In fact, the Bible makes it clear that he was a godly man and a good ruler who did his best to lead the people of Judah toward God:

> *[Hezekiah] removed the high places and broke the sacred pillars, cut down the wooden image and broke in pieces the bronze serpent that Moses had made; for until those days the children of Israel burned incense to it, and called it Nehushtan. He trusted in the Lord God of Israel, so that after him was none like him among all the kings of Judah, nor who were before him.*
>
> 2 KINGS 18:4-5

Hezekiah, who ascended the throne at the age of 25, inspired a period of religious revival in which he was encouraged by Isaiah, perhaps the noblest and most eloquent of the Hebrew prophets. Hezekiah opened the long-closed doors of the temple in Jerusalem and began its renovation, issuing this charge to the priests and Levites:

> *Hear me, Levites! Now sanctify yourselves, sanctify the house of the Lord God of your fathers, and carry out the rubbish from the holy place.*
>
> 2 CHRONICLES 29:5

In short, Hezekiah ushered in a golden age of faith and prosperity for Judah. And if you've bought our culture's notion that good things are supposed to happen to good people, you probably expect that God gave Hezekiah the pleasure of riding off into the sunset after a long, peaceful life.

Alas, that wasn't the case for Hezekiah, just as it's often not the case for people today.

> **Where do you see the philosophy of "Good things should happen to good people" reflected in today's culture?**

> **Do you expect God to bless you with good fortune and good health when you obey Him? Explain.**

A PAINFUL PROPHECY

When Hezekiah was 39 years old, he received terrible news from the prophet Isaiah. It was the kind of news we all fear when sickness comes and we know our body isn't functioning as it should:

> *In those days Hezekiah was sick and near death. And Isaiah the prophet, the son of Amoz, went to him and said to him, "Thus says the LORD: 'Set your house in order, for you shall die and not live.' "*
> ISAIAH 38:1

Maybe you know what it's like to receive that kind of bad news. You've sat in doctors' offices and felt your heart sink as they talked about timetables and treatment options. Or maybe you can only imagine what that would be like.

Either way, it's a terrifying situation—one that Hezekiah wasn't prepared to handle.

> **How do you typically react to bad news?**

In a strange way I find myself encouraged by Hezekiah's reaction to the news:

> *Hezekiah turned his face toward the wall, and prayed to the LORD, and said, "Remember now, O LORD, I pray, how I have walked before You in truth and with a loyal heart, and have done what is good in Your sight." And Hezekiah wept bitterly.*
> ISAIAH 38:2-3

If a godly man like Hezekiah "wept bitterly" (v. 3), we can understand it's no sin to express grief when we're hit with terrible medical news. Hezekiah wasn't just a godly king; he was also human. And humans naturally grieve in the face of bad news.

That means you can too.

How comfortable are you with expressing grief in reaction to bad news or bad situations?

1   2   3   4   5   6   7   8   9   10
Uncomfortable   Comfortable

If you're dealing with an illness, what have you done to grieve and to share your feelings with someone else?

During my illness it took me three days simply to be able to tell my wife the doctor's news. On the day after my diagnosis, she was scheduled to leave town to visit her mother, and I decided not to burden her. I knew she'd immediately cancel her trip—and for what? There was no point in disturbing her until further tests were done.

So I kept my silence. I drove her to the airport the next day, watched her plane vanish into the clouds, and suddenly felt the pangs of loneliness; it was time to confront the dark jungle of my thoughts. I longed for her comfort, but it would be only a three-day wait. We met in another city where I was scheduled to speak, and that's where I quietly told her what the doctors had said.

We wept but not bitterly. Even at such a low moment we knew we had our faith, and we had each other. We held each other for hours as the gray dawn of a new morning gathered outside.

A POIGNANT PRAYER

Even as we grieve, prayer is another appropriate response to the pain of illness or any other negative situation. In fact, it's interesting that Hezekiah prayed *before* he broke down and wept bitterly. He went to God first.

Hezekiah later wrote a memoir of his illness, which is recorded in Isaiah 38:10-15. The first few verses of that passage offer a wrenching picture of Hezekiah's troubled heart. I like the poignancy of these verses in Eugene Peterson's memorable paraphrase:

> *I cry for help until morning.*
> *Like a lion, God pummels and pounds me,*
> *relentlessly finishing me off.*
> *I squawk like a doomed hen,*
>   *moan like a dove.*
> *My eyes ache from looking up for help:*
>   *"Master, I'm in trouble! Get me out of this!"*
> *But what's the use? God himself gave me the word.*
>   *He's done it to me.*
> *I can't sleep—*
>   *I'm that upset, that troubled.*
>
> **ISAIAH 38:13-15, MESSAGE**

Most of us have been in Hezekiah's sandals: "Master, I'm in trouble! Get me out of this!" (v. 14). Even Jesus prayed for the cup to be taken from Him before His crucifixion (see Luke 22:42). But in the end Christ modeled the correct attitude for anyone dealing with painful, confusing circumstances: "Not My will, but Yours, be done" (v. 42).

Take a moment to pray about your current experiences with illness. Record your thoughts as you listen to God and allow Him to minister to you.

Tears and prayer are understandable responses to disease, whether we're the one who's afflicted or the one who's grieving for a loved one. Though we can't predict how the Lord will answer, we know He sees our pain. And that really can be enough.

DAY 3

THE POSSIBILITIES OF DISEASE

On the surface it seems cruelly simple to identify the possible outcomes of illness. When we get sick, it feels as if there are only three things that can happen next: we'll get well, we'll have to deal with the disease (including symptoms and medications) for the rest of our lives, or we'll die.

Obviously, only one of those options is positive in any way. The others underscore why disease is such a common source of fear, frustration, and confusion in our society. When we're sick, it feels as if the best possible outcome is for us to simply get back to normal—and for most of us, normal isn't very exciting.

As we've seen this week, Hezekiah was forced to face the third option for his illness. God told him through the prophet Isaiah that he was going to die in a relatively short period of time.

Hezekiah responded appropriately: he cried out to God and wept bitterly. But as Hezekiah discovered—and as we need to learn—our options during illness aren't as simple as they seem. In God's hands even dreaded diseases come with a number of unforeseen possibilities.

> How would you describe your experiences with God during sickness and other difficult situations?

THE PROMISE

After his prayer and his grief Hezekiah heard another message from God through the prophet Isaiah. This one was much more encouraging:

> *The word of the Lord came to Isaiah, saying, "Go and tell Hezekiah, 'Thus says the Lord, the God of David your father: "I have heard your prayer, I have seen your tears; surely I will add to your days fifteen years." ' "*
> ISAIAH 38:4-5

This was exciting news for Hezekiah! He was no doubt overjoyed to hear that God would reach down from heaven and touch his life in that way. And just to be clear, we're allowed to be happy when God blesses us, especially when His blessings are of the extravagant and supernatural variety.

What are some of the main blessings you've recently received?

Do you feel guilty when God blesses you? Explain.

Why did God do this? Why did he heal the king and give him 15 more years of life? We don't know—not completely. Certainly God wasn't obligated to heal Hezekiah simply because he prayed or because he was the king of Judah.

Here's the truth: nobody has the power to twist God's arm through position or behavior. God is always sovereign, and He always makes decisions based on His wisdom and for His glory. In this case the text suggests that God saw Hezekiah's tears and was moved by compassion. It's really that simple. As Jesus said, God knows how to give good gifts to His children:

> *What man is there among you who, if his son asks for bread, will give him a stone? Or if he asks for a fish, will he give him a serpent? If you then, being evil, know how to give good gifts to your children, how much more will your Father who is in heaven give good things to those who ask Him!*
> MATTHEW 7:9-11

Remember that the next time you feel sick, lonely, depressed, or afraid. God loves you, God wants the best for you, and God may choose to bless you in extravagant ways simply because you asked.

When have you recently asked God for healing? What happened next?

How can we maintain trust in God even if He chooses not to heal us?

I know from experience that God can and does heal our diseases. Yes, my healing came about through doctors and medications—but so did Hezekiah's.

THE PRESCRIPTION

In general, the Bible doesn't give a lot of medical advice. But here's the interesting prescription Hezekiah received from the prophet Isaiah:

> *Isaiah had said, "Let them take a lump of figs, and apply it as a poultice on the boil, and he shall recover."*
> ISAIAH 38:21

Hezekiah's fatal disease stemmed from a boil somewhere on his body. We can assume it had become infected and was leaching poison into his system. God gave Isaiah directions for healing, which were to be passed on to the court physicians attending the king.

You might wonder why God bothered to use the court physicians at all. Why not heal Hezekiah through a simple miracle? But God has a habit of using people, their gifts, and their resources to carry out His plans. In fact, we were created to be God's deputies, doing His work on earth (see Gen. 1:28). Clearly, God used doctors and prescriptions in Hezekiah's time just as He does now.

In what ways have you been blessed by modern medicine and medical techniques?

How much should we credit God for such blessings? Explain.

In 1994 doctors treated my lymphoma with chemotherapy. When the lymphoma returned in 1998, I received a stem-cell transplant. That's the scientific part of the story. But behind the scenes many people were praying for my recovery. That's the faith part of the story.

This raises a question. How much of my healing should be credited to medicine and how much to prayer? We can't know, but it really makes little difference: either way, healing comes from above. We are the ones who draw distinctions between the natural and the supernatural. All of it is God's realm of sovereignty.

Personally, I simply feel blessed to have both available to me: friends on praying knees as well as doctors with skilled hands. Both are wonderful blessings of God.

One positive aspect of medical solutions is that they get us involved. Becoming active agents of God in our own healing process builds our faith by giving us hope. Following the recommendations of my caring and committed doctors was a powerful encouragement to me. I have complete faith that God led me to those specific doctors, and I thank God for them every day.

> **How will you express gratitude and appreciation to God for the medical treatment you receive?**

When we face a serious disease, the first thing we should do is talk to God, asking Him for guidance and healing. Then take advantage of the best medical assistance available, as Hezekiah did. Our God is Jehovah-Rophe—"the LORD who heals you" (Ex. 15:26)— whether He heals us with a miracle, with medicine, or in the world to come.

THE PRAISE

Hezekiah's memoir of his experience with disease continues in Isaiah 38:16-20, where he recorded a testimony of praise to the God who healed him:

> *Indeed it was for my own peace*
> *That I had great bitterness;*
> *But You have lovingly delivered my soul from the pit*
> *   of corruption,*
> *For You have cast all my sins behind Your back.*
> *The LORD was ready to save me;*
> *Therefore we will sing my songs with stringed*
> *   instruments*
> *All the days of our life, in the house of the LORD.*
> ISAIAH 38:17,20

This passage reminds us that after we've recovered from an illness, our first order of business should be to praise God. Some people never think of such a thing; they pray in the time of peril and quickly forget God when they're healed. This neglect reveals not only a lack of consistency but also a lack of gratitude.

How often do you praise God when you recover from illness or difficult situations?

1	2	3	4	5	6	7	8	9	10
Rarely									Always

How will you express gratitude to God for healing you've received?

No illnesses or circumstances are too small for us to bring to God in prayer. It's common for people to thank God when they've experienced a close brush with death, as in a barely missed traffic collision, but far too few of us praise Him after getting over the flu or a migraine headache.

Why should that be? If we can pray about serious illnesses, why shouldn't we pray about all illnesses? Nothing that hurts us is too small for His concern. In fact, Scripture teaches us to pray not just about our health but about everything.

Read the following passages of Scripture and record what they teach about bringing our concerns to God.

1 Thessalonians 5:17

Philippians 4:6-7

If we pray about everything, shouldn't we also praise God in everything? I believe the answer is yes. In fact, the formula for prayer is very simple. When can we pray? All the time. When should we praise God? Whenever we pray.

Whether you're currently experiencing sickness or health, come to God in prayer when you need Him. And no matter how He answers your request, praise Him because of who He is and what He's already done for you.

DAY 4

FEAR PROFILE: NAAMAN

The past century has seen an unprecented number of medical breakthroughs, and I hope we all praise God for that. One result of our increased knowledge is that many diseases have been eliminated or severely reduced across the Western world. Examples include polio, smallpox, tuberculosis, malaria, and typhoid fever.

In spite of our medical success, however, we still have no cure for a number of illnesses. Many forms of cancer are a death sentence, no matter how much chemotherapy or other treatments we're willing to endure. Similarly, we have no cures for illnesses such as HIV/AIDS, lupus, multiple sclerosis, Alzheimer's, and so on.

Which diseases or conditions are you most afraid of? Why?

In the ancient world leprosy was a disease that was universally known and universally feared. The physical symptoms included skin lesions and other deformities. Though not necessarily a fatal illness, leprosy caused numbness in body parts, which often led to secondary infections that could be life-threatening.

But it was the social consequences of leprosy that made it such a terrible and terribly feared disease. For example, look at these commands from the Law of Moses:

> *The leper on whom the sore is, his clothes shall be torn and his head bare; and he shall cover his mustache, and cry, "Unclean! Unclean!" He shall be unclean. All the days he has the sore he shall be unclean. He is unclean, and he shall dwell alone; his dwelling shall be outside the camp.*
> LEVITICUS 13:45-46

What ideas or images come to mind when you hear the word *leper*?

In the ancient world, to be diagnosed with leprosy was to become an outcast from the community. The disease involved a dreadful combination of physical pain, humiliation, shame, and disconnection from society.

What modern diseases carry a social stigma or involve negative relational consequences?

As we continue our exploration of disease and the fear of disease, let's focus on a man who was offered a chance at divine healing from leprosy and who almost rejected that chance because of personal pride.

NAAMAN'S STORY

We're about to explore an Old Testament story of a man who was miraculously healed from a devastating disease. Interestingly, though, the man in question wasn't an Israelite. In fact, he was a leader in a country that oppressed God's people.

Here's how God's Word sets up the story:

> *Naaman, commander of the army of the king of Syria, was a great and honorable man in the eyes of his master, because by him the LORD had given victory to Syria. He was also a mighty man of valor, but a leper. And the Syrians had gone out on raids, and had brought back captive a young girl from the land of Israel. She waited on Naaman's wife.*
>
> 2 KINGS 5:1-2

Why is it significant that Naaman was "a great and honorable man" (v. 1) yet still contracted leprosy?

To make a long story short, when the Israelite servant heard that Naaman had leprosy, she suggested to her mistress that Naaman go and see the prophet Elisha in Samaria, where he could be healed. Naaman decided to go.

From that point on, however, things didn't go as Naaman expected:

Naaman went with his horses and chariot, and he stood at the door of Elisha's house. And Elisha sent a messenger to him, saying, "Go and wash in the Jordan seven times, and your flesh shall be restored to you, and you shall be clean."

2 KINGS 5:9-10

This would have been good news to most people. After all, washing in a river seven times is a small price to pay for being healed from a devastating disease. For Naaman, however, that small price was an affront to his pride:

Naaman became furious, and went away and said, "Indeed, I said to myself, 'He will surely come out to me, and stand and call on the name of the LORD his God, and wave his hand over the place, and heal the leprosy.' Are not the Abanah and the Pharpar, the rivers of Damascus, better than all the waters of Israel? Could I not wash in them and be clean?" So he turned and went away in a rage.

2 KINGS 5:11-12

When have you felt disappointed or angry that God didn't act to heal you or take care of you in the way you expected?

What causes us to place expectations on God?

Fortunately for Naaman, his servant talked some sense into him and convinced him to wash in the Jordan as Elisha had prescribed. As a result, Naaman's "flesh was restored like the flesh of a little child, and he was clean" (v. 14). He was healed.

NAAMAN'S EXAMPLE

We can learn a lot from Naaman's story. First and foremost, we should never turn a blind eye to a reminder that God is sovereign over all forms of sickness. God can heal us, and He often chooses to heal us.

Never forget that.

In a similar way, Naaman's example should remind us that we can't earn healing. As I've ministered to people with severe illnesses and as I think about my own experiences with cancer, I've seen how easy it is to drift into the belief that we must behave better in order to deserve God's attention. Sometimes we can even trick ourselves into thinking if we just become a little more righteous, God will look down on us with favor and end our suffering.

What steps can you take to more fully rely on God for your health and well-being instead of your own efforts?

Finally, Naaman's story reinforces the proper way for us to respond when we experience healing, which is to praise God:

> *[Naaman] returned to the man of God, he and all his aides, and came and stood before him; and he said, "Indeed, now I know that there is no God in all the earth, except in Israel. ... Your servant will no longer offer either burnt offering or sacrifice to other gods, but to the Lord."*
> **2 KINGS 5:15-17**

What steps can you take to continually praise God for the blessings in your life, including your health?

Naaman was "a great and honorable man" (v. 1) who happened to contract a serious disease. He was an enemy of Israel who had a lot to learn about God, but in the end he received both the blessing of physical healing and a spiritual lesson: the God who's sovereign over the universe can certainly heal according to His good purposes.

DAY 5

HOW TO HANDLE DISEASE

We've explored the stories of Hezekiah and Naaman this week, both of whom God healed in miraculous ways. Those are good stories, and they have much to teach us about our God who loves us and wants the best for us.

At the same time, we need to face up to a hard truth that's been implied several times this week but not explicitly stated: there will be times in our lives when we must live with sickness rather than experience healing. There will be times when we fully believe God can heal us, and we can dedicate ourselves to prayer for healing, as Hezekiah did, yet God in His wisdom will choose not to grant our request.

In other words, we won't always get better—not this side of eternity anyway.

> **What's your initial reaction to the previous statement? Why?**

For that reason it's essential for every follower of Christ to learn how to love God and serve His kingdom even in the midst of physical deterioration and disease. Trust me: it can be done. Let's conclude this week's study, then, by examining possible ways to handle disease as a disciple of Jesus.

CENTER YOUR MIND

The human imagination is a powerful force, capable of creating beautiful visions of a desirable future or of conjuring up every worst-case scenario possible. Of course, it's the dark products of our imaginations that can put us in the grip of fear—a place God would never have us go.

We must remember that a sound mind has the power to banish such fears:

> *God has not given us a spirit of fear, but of power and of love and of a sound mind.*
> 2 TIMOTHY 1:7

In another epistle the apostle Paul helped us understand how to achieve and operate with a sound mind:

> The weapons of our warfare are not carnal but mighty in God for pulling down strongholds, casting down arguments and every high thing that exalts itself against the knowledge of God, bringing every thought into captivity to the obedience of Christ.
>
> 2 CORINTHIANS 10:4-5

When we encounter a thought or a worry that pushes us toward fear—"I can't go on!" "I'm going to die!"—we must examine that thought in light of what we know about God. In other words, we must ask ourselves whether the thought has any basis in reality, given our experience of knowing God and the truths of Scripture. If not, we take the thought captive. We don't allow it to run free and lead our imaginations away from God's goodness and toward unhealthy experiences with fear.

What kinds of circumstances often cause you to worry about your health?

How successful are you at "bringing every thought into captivity to the obedience of Christ" (v. 5)?

1	2	3	4	5	6	7	8	9	10
Not successful									Successful

Gaining a sound, centered mind is not as difficult as you may think. If we simply read the Scriptures deeply, thoughtfully, and openly every day, we allow the Holy Spirit to whisper new strength into our thoughts. He alone can tame the reckless power of the human mind. The result will be a mind centered on the truth of God, which is the key to being sustained and not losing heart during hardship.

What obstacles prevent you from reading the Scriptures each day?

Action step 1: This week boost your interaction with the truth of God's Word by reading 1 John 4 several times.

COUNT YOUR BLESSINGS

When you're forced to deal with disease and the fear of illness, make it a point to count your blessings. That's not just good advice; it's a command from God's Word:

> *Rejoice always, pray without ceasing, in everything give thanks; for this is the will of God in Christ Jesus for you.*
> 1 THESSALONIANS 5:16-18

What's your initial reaction to these verses? Why?

I understand if this idea seems like a contradiction to you. After all, how can we possibly feel blessed, let alone count our blessings, in the midst of a debilitating illness?

But what I'm talking about isn't a matter of *feeling* blessed, as if it's something we must conjure up from our imaginations. Rather, it's a matter of seeing the enormous blessings that are already around us. I'm talking about opening our eyes to the wondrous gifts God gives us each day that we often fail to see.

In her book *Gold by Moonlight* Amy Carmichael compares living with pain and disease to a hike through rugged terrain. Even a bleak landscape, she observes, has cheering surprises, like "bright flowers of the edelweiss waiting to be gathered among the rough rocks of difficult circumstances."[4]

What are some tangible blessings you've already received today? Record at least three.

1.

2.

3.

In seasons of sickness our blessings become clearer, richer, and more meaningful. Something therapeutic happens deep in our hearts when we identify those blessings. For example, we can rejoice in the prayers of a friend, in a note from a loved one, in the compassionate care of a conscientious nurse, in a verse from a hymn, in a prescription that lessens our pain, and so on.

Training ourselves to spot these "wildflowers in the wilderness" is the secret to learning to "count it all joy" (Jas. 1:2). This may not be easy, but it's essential to maintaining our spiritual and attitudinal health. It frees us from the tyranny of being limited to a deteriorating physical frame. It's liberating to realize that disease doesn't define who we are—that we're more than our aches and pains.

> Action step 2: Use a journal to record the blessings you encounter this week, paying special attention to positive moments that are unexpected or undeserved.

Remember, the Bible doesn't say we have to be thankful *for* all things, like the pain and discomfort of illness. But it says we should give thanks *in* all things (see 1 Thess. 5:18), including illness. Choose to be thankful that even sickness gives you an opportunity to glorify God.

CONTINUE YOUR WORK

Many Christians know *how* God saves us from our sins—that salvation is by grace through faith (see Eph. 2:8-9). But not all Christians understand *why* God saves us in the first place. Scripture clearly gives us the answer:

> *We are His workmanship, created in Christ Jesus for good works, which God prepared beforehand that we should walk in them.*
> EPHESIANS 2:10

As long as we're on this earth, there's work we can do—work we're called to do. We all have gifts and talents, physical and otherwise, that can be used for the advancement of God's kingdom. And even if we get to the point that we can't walk in the body, we can walk in the Spirit. We can still make a difference for Christ.

That's something the prophet Elisha modeled even on his deathbed.

> Read 2 Kings 13:14-21. What do these verses teach about our usefulness in spite of physical illness?

> Action step 3: Make a list of ways you can work for the advancement of God's kingdom even when you feel your worst.

CONSIDER YOUR FUTURE

One of the most important keys for handling disease in this world is to always remember the breadth and beauty of the world that's yet to come. Paul wrote:

> *I consider that the sufferings of this present time are not worthy to be compared with the glory which shall be revealed in us.*
> ROMANS 8:18

Suppose you won a free trip around the world for you and a loved one. It included first-class accommodations at five-star hotels, private planes, lavish gifts, and personal tours—the works. But also suppose you got a paper cut as you opened the envelope containing the tickets. You might say to your companion, "Oh, I cut my finger!" Maybe you'd grimace for about half a second before grinning from ear to ear and exclaiming, "Who cares? We're about to take the trip of a lifetime!"

I'd never say anything to trivialize sickness and disease; I know the misery of illness firsthand. But according to Paul and from the perspective of our eternal God, the sufferings of this present world are less than a paper cut in relation to the glory yet to be revealed to us.

Although Christ has conquered sin and death, the effects of both still linger. But only temporarily. We must accept disease but only for now—and always with the knowledge that its master, death itself, no longer has power over us (see 1 Cor. 15:54-55).

> Action step 4: Pray throughout this week that God will help you keep an eternal perspective in the midst of sickness and suffering.

Always remember that you're not alone in your struggles with disease. You have a Great Physician who raised His own Son from the dead, leaving behind an empty tomb. You have a heavenly home with welcoming doors open wide. You have a sympathetic Savior who never imparts a spirit of fear but a spirit of power, love, and a sound mind (see 2 Tim. 1:7). To understand and rest in these profound truths allows us to enjoy spiritual health that overcomes even the darkest days that disease can inflict.

1. David Jeremiah, *When Your World Falls Apart* (Nashville: Word, 2000), 38.
2. Ezra Klein, "21 Graphs That Show America's Health-Care Prices Are Ludicrous," *Wonkblog* [online], 26 March 2013 [cited 3 September 2013]. Available from the Internet: *washingtonpost.com.*
3. "U.S. Health Care Costs" [cited 3 September 2013]. Available from the Internet: *kaiseredu.org.*
4. Amy Carmichael, *Gold by Moonlight* (Fort Washington, PA: CLC Publications, 2013).

DEATH: THE FEAR OF DYING

WELCOME BACK TO THIS SMALL-GROUP DISCUSSION
OF WHAT ARE YOU AFRAID OF?

The previous session's application challenge encouraged you to pray for your group members each day throughout the week. Keep those experiences in mind as you answer the following questions.

- Do you find it easy or difficult to pray for others on a regular basis? Explain.
- What tips or methods help you make prayer a regular part of your day?
- How does the act of praying for others affect your conversations with God?

What are the differences between our culture's approach to dealing with disease and the approach outlined in God's Word?

This session will focus on death: the fear of dying. How have you recently been affected by the reality of death?

To prepare for the DVD segment, read aloud the following verses.

> *When this corruptible has put on incorruption, and this mortal has put on immortality, then shall be brought to pass the saying that is written: "Death is swallowed up in victory."*
> *"O Death, where is your sting?*
> *O Hades, where is your victory?"*
> *The sting of death is sin, and the strength of sin is the law. But thanks be to God, who gives us the victory through our Lord Jesus Christ.*
> 1 CORINTHIANS 15:54-57

WATCH

THE FACT OF DEATH
Psalm 116:15

THE FACES OF DEATH
1. _____ death

   In physical death the spirit and soul leave the _____ and move either into the presence of God or to isolation from God.

2. _____ death

   Spiritual death is the separation of the natural man from _____.

3. _____ death

   The second death is the final _____ from God and the final misery of the wicked in hell following the great white throne judgment at the end of the millennium.

   If you have been born only once, you will have to die _____. But if you have been born twice, you will have to die only _____.

THE FEAR OF DEATH
1. The prince of death has been _____.

   Because Christ died, we have lives that are _____. Because Christ arose, we have lives that are _____.

2. The power of death has been _____.
3. The process of death has been _____.
4. The picture of death has been _____.

TRUTHS ABOUT DEATH FROM PSALM 23
1. Death is a _____, not a destination.
2. Death is a _____, not a reality.
3. Death is lonely, but you're never _____.

   You can face death with your faith if you will put your faith in _____ _____.

RESPOND

*USE THE FOLLOWING QUESTIONS TO DISCUSS
THE DVD SEGMENT WITH YOUR GROUP.*

What did you find interesting or surprising in Dr. Jeremiah's teaching?

How would you summarize our culture's response to the reality of death?

How do you typically react to the reality and certainty of death?

What questions do you have about the distinctions made between physical death, spiritual death, and second death?

Respond to Dr. Jeremiah's statement: "When Jesus stepped from the open tomb on Resurrection Sunday, Satan's defeat was certain. His weapon of death had been destroyed. Because Christ died, we have lives that are forgiven. Because Christ arose, we have lives that are forever."

What messages should we as Christians communicate about death to the culture around us? How can we seek opportunities to share those messages more often?

APPLICATION. This week look for ways our culture attempts to minimize the reality of death. When you encounter an example, take a moment to pray that God will grant you opportunities to share the truth about death and your hope for eternal life with those who need to hear it.

THIS WEEK'S SCRIPTURE MEMORY. Use the memory card at the back of the book to memorize this verse:

> *Yea, though I walk through the valley of the shadow
>   of death,
> I will fear no evil;
> For You are with me;
> Your rod and Your staff, they comfort me.*
>
> PSALM 23:4

ASSIGNMENT. Read week 5 and complete the activities before the next group experience. Consider going deeper into this content by reading chapter 9 in Dr. Jeremiah's book *What Are You Afraid Of?* (Tyndale, 2013).

Video sessions available for purchase at *www.lifeway.com/afraid*

WASTING OUR BREATH

Death. I know that's not your favorite subject. It's not mine either, and I'm not trying to cloud your day by bringing it up. But I want to point out that for many people, death is both the ultimate fear and the ultimate confusion. When someone dies, I hear a lot of people say, "He's in a better place," even though they'd previously been trying with all their might to pray that person away from that place.

Woody Allen once said, "It's not that I'm afraid of dying, I just don't want to be there when it happens."[1] Apparently he's given the matter some thought, because he also made this comment: "I don't want to achieve immortality through my work; I want to achieve it through not dying. I don't want to live on in the hearts of my countrymen; I want to live on in my apartment."[2]

Most of us treat death as the ultimate obscene word. Rather than simply saying, "He died," we plug in an endless supply of euphemisms: "Passed on." "Went to a better place." "Was called home." "Went to sleep." "Departed this life." Or if Shakespeare is your thing, "shuffled off this mortal coil."[3] John Betjeman wrote:

> Oh why do people waste their breath
> Inventing dainty names for death?[4]

Right about now you may be thinking about skipping to next week's study, hoping it will address a more manageable fear. I feel your trepidation. Having brushed against the specter of death myself because of serious illness, I'm not motivated to dwell on the subject any more than I have to.

But what if I promised you that you could forever change the way you look at death, maybe even move it out of the fear category entirely? After all, wouldn't you say the fear of death is taking up too much space in your anxiety closet?

I think it's the idea of facing the unknown that frightens people. So let's take on this subject of death head on. With the Bible as our guide, I firmly believe we can pull death out of the terrifying darkness and bring it into the light once and for all.

1. Eric Lax, *Woody Allen: A Biography* (Cambridge, MA: Da Capo Press, 1991), 26.
2. Woody Allen [cited 16 September 2013]. Available from the Internet: *izquotes.com*.
3. William Shakespeare, *Hamlet*, act 3, scene 1.
4. John Betjeman, "Churchyards," *Faith and Doubt of John Betjeman: An Anthology of His Religious Verse*, ed. Kevin J. Gardner (London: Continuum, 2005), 77.

DAY 1

THE FACT OF DEATH

On February 1, 2003, the space shuttle *Columbia* attempted to reenter Earth's atmosphere after its 28th mission in space. The attempt wasn't successful. The shuttle broke apart around nine o'clock in the morning, resulting in the deaths of seven astronauts.

Subsequent investigations discovered that a piece of insulating foam the size of a small briefcase had peeled off during the shuttle's launch 16 days earlier and punctured one of the vessel's wings. The intense heat of reentry caused gases to penetrate the wing, triggering the catastrophe that killed everyone on board.

> **What recent events forced our culture as a whole to admit or examine the reality of death?**

> **In what ways were you affected by those events?**

Several years after the *Columbia* tragedy, a poignant report emerged that shed new light on the incident. While the mission was in progress, NASA scientists became aware that a piece of foam had struck the shuttle during the launch, and they worked to determine whether the impact would have any negative consequences during the shuttle's reentry. Specifically, they attempted to discern whether the damage was fatal.

Wayne Hale, the space shuttle program manager, recalls these words of flight director Jon Harpold:

> There is nothing we can do about damage to the TPS [thermal protection system]. If it has been damaged it's probably better not to know. I think the crew would rather not know. Don't you think it would be better for them to have a happy successful flight and die unexpectedly during entry than to stay on orbit, knowing that there was nothing to be done, until the air ran out?[1]

Harpold's question was merely speculative, and NASA later determined (erroneously) that *Columbia*'s reentry would be safe. The shuttle crew was given a full report of NASA's conclusion, and no one on the ship or on the ground had any expectation that the damage would prove fatal.

Still, it's a haunting question: What would you do if you knew the shuttle crew was doomed to die? Would you tell them the truth, causing indescribable mental anguish but giving them time to say their good-byes, reflect on life, and perhaps make peace with God? Or would you remain silent, making their final hours a time of exhilaration and anticipation of reunion with their loved ones?

How would you handle the situation described?

In a way, the plight of *Columbia* resembles our own experiences: we're flying through space on a spinning planet, and every person is subject to sudden death at any moment. None of us will escape. The difference is, we all know we're going to die, and we have the opportunity to prepare. So let's prepare. Instead of running away from the inevitability of death, let's explore what the Bible has to say about this common source of fear.

What practical, legal, or financial steps have you taken to prepare for your death?

What spiritual steps have you taken to prepare for your death?

THE BEGINNING OF THE END

The Bible isn't afraid to speak of death or to call it what it is. In fact, the words *die* and *death* occur nearly nine hundred times in the New King James Version of God's Word.

The Bible pulls no punches, making it clear that all people will experience death:

> *As it is appointed for men to die once, but after this the judgment,*
> *so Christ was offered once to bear the sins of many.*
> HEBREWS 9:27-28

In the same way, there are a number of occasions when the Bible gives voice to our human fears about death. For example, last week we looked at Hezekiah's forlorn, frightened reaction to the news of his imminent death. Even David expressed strong apprehension about the end of his life:

> *What profit is there in my blood,*
> *When I go down to the pit?*
> *Will the dust praise You?*
> *Will it declare Your truth?*
> *Hear, O Lᴏʀᴅ, and have mercy on me;*
> *Lᴏʀᴅ, be my helper!*
> PSALM 30:9-10

From the time of Adam's fall in Genesis 3, the Bible presents death as a natural and inevitable part of human life. Indeed, the countdown to death begins at birth, so you and I are dying at this very moment.

What's your response to the previous statements?

On the whole, however, the Bible offers a surprisingly redemptive view of death. Yes, God's Word makes it clear that death is a reality we all must face, but the Scriptures often describe death in a way that's more comforting than regretful.

Read the following passages of Scripture and describe how each characterizes the experience of death.

Genesis 25:7-10

2 Kings 22:20

I consider the following to be the most beautiful verse in the Bible about the death of God's people:

> *Precious in the sight of the L*ORD
> *Is the death of His saints.*
> **PSALM 116:15**

This verse and others point to a paradox we need to understand as followers of Jesus: although death begins the moment we're born, eternal life also begins the moment we're born again by the Spirit of God through faith in Christ.

What ideas or images come to mind when you hear the phrase
eternal life?

How would you define or describe the eternal life we've been offered
through faith in Christ?

THE TRUTH ABOUT ETERNAL LIFE

Many Christians have the mistaken notion that eternal life begins when they die—that we somehow step into eternal life once our physical bodies perish and our souls are set free. But such ideas aren't biblically accurate.

Instead, eternal life begins when we're born again into the kingdom of God. That's what Jesus taught:

> *Jesus spoke these words, lifted up His eyes to heaven, and said:*
> *"Father, the hour has come. Glorify Your Son, that Your Son also*
> *may glorify You, as You have given Him authority over all flesh,*
> *that He should give eternal life to as many as You have given*
> *Him. **And this is eternal life, that they may know You, the only***
> ***true God, and Jesus Christ whom You have sent.***"
> **JOHN 17:1-3, EMPHASIS ADDED**

I hope you realize what this means. If you have a relationship with God through Jesus Christ, then you're experiencing eternal life right now even though you haven't physically died. And if you're experiencing eternal life right now, death is no more than a brief interruption in the life you're already experiencing—a life that has no end.

How does the reality that you're already experiencing eternal life influence your perspective on death?

Many other passages in the New Testament confirm this view of death as something temporary and transitional, including the following.

> *He said to Jesus, "Lord, remember me when You come into Your kingdom." And Jesus said to him, "Assuredly, I say to you, today you will be with Me in Paradise."*
>
> LUKE 23:42-43

> *We know that if our earthly house, this tent, is destroyed, we have a building from God, a house not made with hands, eternal in the heavens. For in this we groan, earnestly desiring to be clothed with our habitation which is from heaven, if indeed, having been clothed, we shall not be found naked. For we who are in this tent groan, being burdened, not because we want to be unclothed, but further clothed, that mortality may be swallowed up by life.*
>
> 2 CORINTHIANS 5:1-4

How do these verses affect your understanding of death and eternal life?

The Bible, then, gives us the full truth about death. It isn't something to fear but a journey begun at birth that brings us to our final destination: being with Christ for all eternity.

That sounds like good news to me.

DAY 2

THE FACES OF DEATH

In today's world most people believe we're all talking about the same phenomenon when we speak of or witness death. But that's actually not true. Over decades of ministry, I've sat in enough hospital rooms and next to enough deathbeds to understand that death can wear many different faces.

For example, some people see death as a terrifying monster that's hot on their heels in pursuit and never willing to give up the chase. Others see death as a welcome stranger who's come to escort them home. And between those two extremes are many shades or faces of death.

> **What emotions do you experience when you contemplate the reality of your death? Why?**

I think the way we respond to death in our last moments—frightened or calm, panicked or at peace—has a lot to do with the type of death we expect to experience. Yes, there's more than one face of death.

Let's continue exploring our fear of death by gaining a firm understanding of the three types of death outlined in God's Word: physical death, spiritual death, and second death.

1. PHYSICAL DEATH

The word *death* literally means *separation*. With that definition in mind, the best way to understand the concept of physical death is to categorize it as the separation of a person's spirit from the physical body.

This is what James referred to when he said:

> *As the body without the spirit is dead, so faith without works is dead also.*
> JAMES 2:26

Solomon's description of physical death is both accurate and poetic:

> *Remember your Creator before the silver cord is loosed,*
> *Or the golden bowl is broken,*
> *Or the pitcher shattered at the fountain,*
> *Or the wheel broken at the well.*
> *Then the dust will return to the earth as it was,*
> *And the spirit will return to God who gave it.*
> **ECCLESIASTES 12:6-7**

In physical death the spirit and the soul leave the body and move either into the presence of God or into isolation from God. There are no exceptions; the statistics on death are 100 percent, with the possible exception of Christians who will be alive at the moment of the rapture (see 1 Thess. 4:16-17). As the saying goes, death is still the number one killer in the world.

What's the closest you've come to witnessing someone's death?

How were you affected by that experience?

2. SPIRITUAL DEATH

The idea of spiritual death refers to another kind of separation: our separation from God. Because of our sin we've fallen short of the glory of God (see Rom. 3:23) and severed the possibility of a relationship with Him based on our own merit. Even though we're physically alive, we experience a spiritual separation from God that the Bible describes as a kind of death:

> *The wages of sin is death, but the gift of God is eternal life in Christ Jesus our Lord.*
> **ROMANS 6:23**

When God warned Adam and Eve about the consequences of sin, He referred to both physical and spiritual death:

The Lord God commanded the man, saying, "Of every tree of the garden you may freely eat; but of the tree of the knowledge of good and evil you shall not eat, for in the day that you eat of it you shall surely die."

GENESIS 2:16-17

Adam and Eve didn't die physically when they ate the forbidden fruit, although their bodies began the process of death at that moment. But Adam and Eve did experience spiritual death immediately after their sin. They were separated from God.

Sadly, the same is true for us:

... just as through one man sin entered the world, and death through sin, and thus death spread to all men, because all sinned.

ROMANS 5:12

Thankfully, our spiritual death doesn't have to remain a permanent condition. We've already seen in Romans 6:23 that "the gift of God is eternal life in Christ Jesus our Lord." Jesus' death and resurrection grant us victory over physical and spiritual death and make it possible for us to experience eternal life.

How would you summarize the concept of spiritual death?

3. SECOND DEATH

The last form of death, second death, is final banishment from God—the final misery of the wicked in hell following the great white throne judgment (see Rev. 20:11) at the end of the millennium. John described this second death in the Book of Revelation:

The sea gave up the dead who were in it, and Death and Hades delivered up the dead who were in them. And they were judged, each one according to his works. Then Death and Hades were cast into the lake of fire. This is the second death. And anyone not found written in the Book of Life was cast into the lake of fire.

REVELATION 20:13-15

What are your initial reactions to this passage? Why?

In essence the second death is the separation of our eternal souls from God. And the terrible news is that this separation lasts for all eternity.

I often try to bring understanding to this subject by using a mathematical formula: if you've been born only once, you'll have to die twice. But if you've been born twice, you'll have to die only once. And that's good news!

How should the reality of the second death influence our earthly goals and choices?

I must note that death also brings about another kind of separation: the separation from loved ones, which we feel physically, spiritually, and emotionally. In truth this is another primary reason so many people are terrified of death: they dread the idea of being separated from the people they care about most.

What do you miss most about your friends and family members who've died?

Here's the bottom line: as followers of Christ, we should have a radically different perspective on death. We should think differently than the world does about our own spiritual conditions and the people left behind when death occurs.

We should understand that, for Christians, the many forms of separation caused by death are all temporary. Yes, it's appropriate for us to mourn the deaths of our loved ones and even to feel a touch of apprehension at the thought of our own separation from this world. But in the end we should hold fast to the knowledge that Christ has already secured our ultimate victory over the grave.

Let's remember that. Let's allow our souls to be kindled by the eternal hope of reunion with those we've lost, after which there will be no more parting.

DAY 3

THE FEAR OF DEATH

Have you heard of *thanatophobia?* It's a medical term that refers to the abnormal fear of death—and the word *abnormal* is important in that definition. People who suffer from *thanatophobia* are so afraid of death that it impairs their ability to live a normal life. They're paralyzed by the thought of dying.

Obviously, *thanatophobia* is a rare condition that most of us will never deal with. But I think we can empathize with those who do. I think most of us can at least imagine what it might be like to be paralyzed by the fear of death, because most of us have been threatened or hindered to a smaller degree by that same fear.

> How have you been threatened or hindered by the fear of death?

The truth is that many Christians live with a genuine fear of death. They don't want to think about it. They don't want to talk about it. They'd rather pretend it doesn't exist, both for themselves and the people they love.

I believe this attitude toward death reveals a spiritual problem that's subtly affected believers throughout the church. So I'd like to spend today examining several biblical reasons we as followers of Christ shouldn't be afraid of death.

Indeed, if you're a Christian who remains apprehensive about death, even a little, I want to encourage you to replace your fear with biblical hope and assurance. I pray that the biblical truths presented here will help you move toward faith in Christ so that His life brings you to joyful anticipation of the future, in spite of your inevitable death.

> In what ways do you need hope right now?

> In what ways do you need assurance about the future?

THE PRINCE OF DEATH HAS BEEN DEFEATED

From the first sin in the garden of Eden until Jesus' sacrificial death for our sins, the Devil used death to gain the upper hand and enjoy the last laugh. Satan stirred in people the desire to violate God's laws and then watched them reap death as the reward for their sin. Paul wrote:

> *The sting of death is sin, and the strength of sin is the law.*
> **1 CORINTHIANS 15:56**

It was quite a system. We failed to be obedient, and we died for it—every time.

Thankfully, Jesus set us free from that terrible cycle. Indeed, the author of the Book of Hebrews declared that Jesus used His own death to conquer death. And in doing so, He freed us not only from the power of death but also from the fear of death:

> *Inasmuch then as the children have partaken of flesh and blood, He Himself likewise shared in the same, that through death He might destroy him who had the power of death, that is, the devil, and release those who through fear of death were all their lifetime subject to bondage.*
> **HEBREWS 2:14-15**

In His death and resurrection the Son of God played the Devil's own trump card. Just as David used the sword of Goliath to cut off the giant's head, Jesus used Satan's own weapon, death, to defeat the Devil and to guarantee victory.

Where have you seen people in today's culture "all their lifetime subject to bondage" (v. 15) because of the fear of death?

Do you feel released from bondage to the fear of death? Explain.

When Jesus stepped from the open tomb on Resurrection Sunday, Satan's defeat was certain. His weapon of death had been destroyed. Although he's still alive and active, his failure is a foregone conclusion. He must settle for winning the smaller battles, because the war he started has been lost forever.

Satan's last hope is to convince you to live as if the victory of Christ never happened. He'd love for you to remain enslaved to the fear of death. As followers of Christ, we must resist that fear.

> Read James 4:7-8. What steps can you take to resist Satan and fight against the bondage that comes from the fear of death?

Always remember these two important truths:

1. Because Christ died, we're *forgiven*.
2. Because Christ rose from the grave, we live *forever*.

THE POWER OF DEATH HAS BEEN DESTROYED

One of the main ways to fight against the fear of death is to embrace the hope we're continually offered in God's Word. For example, I love this outburst of hope from the prophet Isaiah:

> *He will swallow up death forever,*
> *And the Lord GOD will wipe away tears from all faces;*
> *The rebuke of His people*
> *He will take away from all the earth;*
> *For the LORD has spoken.*
>
> ISAIAH 25:8

Hosea, a contemporary of Isaiah, also foretold Christ's victory over death:

> *I will ransom them from the power of the grave;*
> *I will redeem them from death.*
> *O Death, I will be your plagues!*
> *O Grave, I will be your destruction!*
>
> HOSEA 13:14

> How do these passages inspire you to hope?

These Old Testament passages pointed to Jesus' coming sacrifice and resurrection as a primary source of our hope. Christ came to "ransom" His people from the grave and to "redeem" us from the power of death (Hos. 13:14). Both terms refer to paying a price in order to set a slave or a prisoner free. Jesus paid the price for our sins through His own death, so we no longer have to be terrified by our inability to pay that price.

The New Testament clarified God's ultimate victory over death not only by providing the details of Jesus' saving work but also by pointing us to the reality of life after death. Because of passages like this one from the Book of John, you can rest assured that the end of your physical life won't be the end of *you:*

> *Let not your heart be troubled; you believe in God, believe also in Me. In My Father's house are many mansions; if it were not so, I would have told you. I go to prepare a place for you. And if I go and prepare a place for you, I will come again and receive you to Myself; that where I am, there you may be also.*
> JOHN 14:1-3

Read the following passages of Scripture and record what they teach about eternal life with God in heaven.

Romans 8:38-39

Hebrews 11:13-16

Revelation 21:1-5

For those of us who follow Christ and live for Him, death has become nothing more than a doorway into His presence. Why would we fear such a gift?

How will you intentionally reject the fear of death in the weeks, months, and years to come?

There are only two ways to face the future: with fear or with faith. Those who live by faith in the Son of God (see Gal. 2:20) will find all their fears—especially the fear of death—consumed by the security of His person and the certainty of His promises. May this be true in your life today.

DAY 4

FEAR PROFILE: PAUL

According to folk wisdom and down-to-earth good sense, one of the best ways to combat fear is to face it. Especially as kids, we're constantly told to face our fear, which usually means we're supposed to seek controlled experiences with whatever we're afraid of in order to overcome our anxiety.

For example, if someone's afraid of the dark, they're often encouraged to intentionally spend time in darkness to overcome that fear. Or if someone's thrown off a horse while learning to ride, they're usually encouraged to get back in the saddle and try again.

> **When have you attempted to face your fears by exposing yourself to what you were afraid of?**

> **Has this method of combating fear been successful for you? Explain.**

Obviously, it won't work for us to seek an experience with death in order to combat the fear of death. We can't face this fear that way. But we can learn from the experiences of others. And with the exception of Jesus Christ, no person in the Scriptures had as much practical and emotional experience with death as the apostle Paul.

STICKS AND STONES

Most of us remember the apostle Paul as a spiritual giant and a great man of God, and he was. But there were two periods in Paul's life. Before his conversion Paul (known as Saul at the time) was a zealous, often ruthless figure who became familiar with death for all the wrong reasons.

For example, Paul was present at the stoning of Stephen, who was the first person to be martyred in the name of Christ (see Acts 7:54-60).

Later Paul became a leading participant in the Jewish establishment's violent attempts to suppress the growing church:

> *As for Saul, he made havoc of the church, entering every house, and dragging off men and women, committing them to prison.*
> ACTS 8:3

> *Saul, still breathing threats and murder against the disciples of the Lord, went to the high priest and asked letters from him to the synagogues of Damascus, so that if he found any who were of the Way, whether men or women, he might bring them bound to Jerusalem.*
> ACTS 9:1-2

Fortunately, God intervened. Paul was converted to Christianity through a miraculous experience with Christ, and he went on to plant churches throughout the ancient world and to write much of the New Testament.

Read Acts 9:1-9. What do these verses teach about God?

How do these verses help you understand Paul?

Given Paul's earlier experiences with violence and persecution, it's both unfortunate and ironic that Paul's efforts to spread the gospel resulted in his own persecution, even to the point of death.

Look at what happened to Paul in the city of Lystra, for example:

> *Jews from Antioch and Iconium came there; and having persuaded the multitudes, they stoned Paul and dragged him out of the city, supposing him to be dead. However, when the disciples gathered around him, he rose up and went into the city. And the next day he departed with Barnabas to Derbe.*
> ACTS 14:19-20

Most scholars believe Paul didn't actually die and rise from the dead, given that the text takes pains to avoid making that claim. But he certainly came close. The practice of stoning was relatively common in those days; a group of people smashed a victim with rocks until he or she died. Death was the goal, and the fact that Paul escaped with his life should be seen as another miracle of God.

That wasn't the only time Paul's life was on the line during his earthly service to God. He was also shipwrecked three times, beaten with rods on multiple occasions, whipped, and jailed.

> Read 2 Corinthians 11:22-29. How did these experiences contribute to Paul's understanding of death and the fear of death?

Paul also encountered death during a surprising incident involving a young man named Eutychus. Paul was preaching a sermon late into the night when something terrible and unexpected occurred:

> *In a window sat a certain young man named Eutychus, who was sinking into a deep sleep. He was overcome by sleep; and as Paul continued speaking, he fell down from the third story and was taken up dead. But Paul went down, fell on him, and embracing him said, "Do not trouble yourselves, for his life is in him."*
> ACTS 20:9-10

What a strange and miraculous occurrence! Most of us can certainly empathize with the young man who fell asleep during a long sermon, but it must have been a tragedy to see him perish after his fall. And a rush of awe and worship must have followed when God's power over death was revealed once more and the young man walked away from the incident in one piece.

> When have you recently been reminded of God's power over death?

All in all, Paul witnessed the murders of others, expected to die himself on numerous occasions, and was always prepared to do so. He watched a friend die and then return to life. Therefore, Paul was imminently qualified to speak about death and the fear it so often produces in our lives. Let's examine what he said on this subject.

TO STAY OR GO

Paul was in prison when he wrote the Book of Philippians, among other epistles—another situation in which he was forced to contemplate the possibility of his death. We know this is true because he included some of those thoughts in the letter itself:

> *To me, to live is Christ, and to die is gain. But if I live on in the flesh, this will mean fruit from my labor; yet what I shall choose I cannot tell. For I am hard-pressed between the two, having a desire to depart and be with Christ, which is far better. Nevertheless to remain in the flesh is more needful for you. And being confident of this, I know that I shall remain and continue with you all for your progress and joy of faith, that your rejoicing for me may be more abundant in Jesus Christ by my coming to you again.*
>
> **PHILIPPIANS 1:21-26**

What are your initial reactions to this passage?

How would you summarize Paul's message in these verses?

Make sure you understand what Paul was contemplating in these verses. Most scholars agree that Paul was writing this letter during his first imprisonment (A.D. 60–62), which means he wasn't yet confined in the infamous Mamertine dungeon in Rome. Even so, Paul was very much aware that Christians were being persecuted throughout the ancient world, especially since Paul had participated in that persecution years earlier.

Paul believed his life was in jeopardy, and he used his letter to contemplate a simple yet poignant question: Would it be better for me to live or to die?

Surprisingly, Paul decided he would be more than OK with dying. He was "hard-pressed" by the choice, but in the end he believed dying and departing this world would be "far better" (v. 23) because it would lead him to Christ.

Later, when Paul was confined in the terrible Mamertine dungeon in Rome, he wrote another letter to Timothy, one of his protégés in ministry. By this time Paul was old, physically beaten down, and betrayed by the people closest to him. He was alone, and he knew he was about to die at the hands of the Roman authorities.

Even so, his belief in the inherent blessing of death was unchanged:

> *I am already being poured out as a drink offering, and the time of my departure is at hand. I have fought the good fight, I have finished the race, I have kept the faith. Finally, there is laid up for me the crown of righteousness, which the Lord, the righteous Judge, will give to me on that Day, and not to me only but also to all who have loved His appearing.*
> 2 TIMOTHY 4:6-8

> *The Lord will deliver me from every evil work and preserve me for His heavenly kingdom. To Him be glory forever and ever. Amen!*
> 2 TIMOTHY 4:18

How do these verses contribute to your understanding of life and what it means to follow Christ?

How do they contribute to your understanding of death?

As Christians, we're blessed with the knowledge that death is nothing more than an open door into the presence of Jesus. We need not be afraid.

DAY 5

HOW TO PREPARE FOR DEATH

An 11-year-old once wrote to Pope John Paul II with this question: "What is it like when you die? Nobody will tell me. I just want to know, but I don't want to do it."[2] I think we can all relate!

What questions would you most like to have answered about the process of death?

What have you learned about death during this week's study?

Being curious about death isn't limited to 11-year-olds. Most people have a number of questions about the process of death, even if we rarely verbalize them to others. *How will it happen for me? What will it feel like? Will it hurt?* And most importantly, *What will happen to me after I die?*

Such questions aren't morbid or inappropriate. They're natural, because the simple fact is that all of us will die. There will come a time when your body fails and you pass from this physical life on earth into the afterlife.

Unfortunately, the Bible doesn't provide many details about that passing. But it does help us prepare for it. Look at this verse, for example:

> *Yea, though I walk through the valley of the shadow
>   of death,
> I will fear no evil;
> For You are with me;
> Your rod and Your staff, they comfort me.*
> PSALM 23:4

What are your initial reactions to this passage?

The sheer beauty of the passage never fails to move me. But the power of this verse can also help us prepare for what we often fear. When we face death—our own or the death of a loved one—we should hold this verse close to our hearts. It's poetic, yes, but it also teaches us some important principles about how to prepare for the end of life.

DEATH IS A JOURNEY

In this shepherd psalm David saw death not as a destination but as a journey through a dark country—a journey we make with God's hand in ours. My friend Rob Morgan describes how this journey reveals the transitory nature of death:

> Psalm 23:4 does not speak of a cave or a dead-end trail. It's a valley, which means it has an opening on both ends. ... The emphasis is on *through*, which indicates a temporary state, a transition, a brighter path ahead, a hopeful future. For Christians, problems are always temporary and blessings always eternal (as opposed to non-Christians, whose blessings are temporal and whose problems are eternal). Valleys don't go on forever, and the road ahead is always bright for the child of God, as bright as His promises. There are no cul-de-sacs on His maps, no blind alleys in His will, no dead ends in His guidance.[3]

One way we prepare for death is to solidify our belief that death isn't final but temporary. It's not a climax or an ending but merely a journey from one reality to another—from an imperfect home to a perfect one.

How can you move from intellectually understanding this view of death to firmly believing it in your heart?

Of course, believing that death is a part of the journey will be a comfort to us only if we know the final destination of the journey is eternal life in heaven. If we're destined for eternal separation from God in hell, then death will be and should be a terrifying reality.

The most important step in preparing for death, then, is to ensure that your salvation is secure through the death and resurrection of Jesus Christ.

> **Action step 1:** If you feel unsure in any way about your salvation and eternal security in Christ, take immediate steps to resolve that uncertainty. Talk with your pastor or a mature Christian friend and make things right with God.

Most of us speak of hope for the afterlife. But the way we approach death shows what we really believe. Those committed to a biblical perspective have no reason to treat death as their greatest enemy. Instead, they see it as another journey that calls for preparation. They say their good-byes, get their affairs in order, and prepare their spirits for the joy of a new existence.

DEATH IS A SHADOW

Donald Grey Barnhouse was driving home from the funeral of his first wife, and he and his children were overcome with grief. As he sought a word of comfort for his kids, a huge moving van passed them, and its shadow swept over the car.

Barnhouse thought for a moment, then said, "Children, would you rather be run over by a truck or by its shadow?"

"Of course, Dad, we'd much rather be run over by the shadow!" the children said. "That can't hurt us at all."

"Two thousand years ago," the father replied, "the truck of death ran over the Lord Jesus … in order that only its shadow might run over us."[4]

> **What are the elements of death that make it painful and difficult for us to bear?**

David wrote, "Yea, though I walk through the valley of the *shadow* of death" (Ps. 23:4, emphasis added). And the wonderful news is that shadows are only the deflection of light. They can frighten, but they can do no real harm.

For a Christian, death is only a shadow. No longer is it the true substance of our fear; rather, it's just a momentary obscuring of the light. That's why Jesus' promise to every believer is so powerful: "Because I live, you will live also" (John 14:19).

In a similar way, Jesus reminded us that His death and resurrection are the reasons death exists only as a shadow for those of us who follow Him:

> Jesus said to her, "I am the resurrection and the life. He who believes in Me, though he may die, he shall live. And whoever lives and believes in Me shall never die. Do you believe this?"
> JOHN 11:25-26

Jesus' words are wonderful news, yet at the same time they remind us that not everyone accepts His incredible offer of eternal life. Some people experience death without believing in Jesus. As a result, their friends and family members who are left behind can experience incredible pain.

As Christians, we aren't able to trust Jesus on behalf of those we love. But we aren't helpless either. One of the best ways to prepare for the eventual deaths of those we care about is to consistently pray for their salvation, asking God to send His Spirit again and again to convict them of their sin and draw them to Him.

> Action step 2: Make a list of friends and family members who may still need to accept Jesus' gift of salvation. Commit to pray for those individuals each day.

> How can you find opportunities to share the gospel with the people in your life who need to hear it?

DEATH CAN BE LONELY, BUT WE'RE NEVER ALONE

I love the simple comfort of David's words, spoken to God:

> You are with me;
> Your rod and Your staff, they comfort me.
> PSALM 23:4

There's a narrative change in Psalm 23 that's easy to miss unless you're looking for it. In the first three verses David referred to the Lord in the third person: "He makes me to lie down" (v. 2). "He leads" (v. 2). "He restores" (v. 3).

Very abruptly, however, third person becomes second person in verse 4. David said, *"You* are with me" (emphasis added). He stopped talking *about* the Shepherd and began talking *to* Him. It's as if he'd been talking about God and then, in the midst of the shadows, realized God was right there:

> *I will fear no evil;*
> *For You are with me.*
>
> **PSALM 23:4**

In other words, what began as an essay became an intimate conversation.

It all makes beautiful sense if you've ever walked through that valley. You think about God, and suddenly you find yourself caught up in a conversation with Him. His presence suddenly changes your whole line of thought. In fact, I've spoken with many people who were traveling their darkest roads, and they've often told me they were never more aware of the presence of the Shepherd than when they were walking in that shadow.

How have you experienced God's presence during difficult times?

I've counseled many people as they sat in death's waiting room, and experience has proved to me that God makes His presence known as they walk through the valley. He reaches for their hands. He whispers words of comfort and promise. And it's not limited just to the dying people themselves; it's also for those who grieve their loss. They too walk through the valley, and God reaches out to them in their pain.

Action step 3: When it's appropriate, begin preparing your loved ones for your eventual death. Plainly speak with them about your trust in Christ, your inheritance as God's child, and your hope for eternal life in His presence.

For Christians, death isn't the end of our lives. It's not the end of anything, really, but the beginning of our eternal destiny in the presence of God.

1. Wayne Hale, "After 10 Years: Working on the Wrong Problem" [13 January 2013, cited 16 September 2013]. Available from the Internet: *http://waynehale.wordpress.com*.
2. Nino Lo Bello, *The Incredible Book of Vatican Facts and Papal Curiosities* (Liguori, MO: Liguori Publications, 1998), 16.
3. Robert J. Morgan, *The Lord Is My Shepherd* (New York: Howard Books, 2013), 116–17.
4. Michael P. Green, ed., *Illustrations for Biblical Preaching* (Grand Rapids, MI: Baker Book House, 1989), 91.

DEITY: THE FEAR OF GOD

*WELCOME BACK TO THIS SMALL-GROUP DISCUSSION
OF* WHAT ARE YOU AFRAID OF?

The previous session's application challenge encouraged you to pray for and seek opportunities to share the biblical view of death with those who need to hear it. If you're comfortable, share what was interesting about your experiences.

How would you describe the connection between thinking about death and thinking about God?

We've covered five fears throughout this study so far: failure, depression, loneliness, disease, and death. Which of these fears has affected you most? Why?

This session will focus on deity: the fear of God. What ideas or images come to mind when you hear the phrase *fear of God?*

To prepare for the DVD segment, read aloud the following verses.

> *By the word of the L*ORD *the heavens were made,
> And all the host of them by the breath of His mouth.
> He gathers the waters of the sea together as a heap;
> He lays up the deep in storehouses.
> Let all the earth fear the L*ORD*;
> Let all the inhabitants of the world stand in awe of Him.
> For He spoke, and it was done;
> He commanded, and it stood fast.*
>
> **PSALM 33:6-9**

WATCH

COMPLETE THE VIEWER GUIDE BELOW AS YOU WATCH DVD SESSION 6.

It's the lack of this discussion of the fear of God that contributes to the _____ into which this world is rapidly descending.

The definition of the fear of God extends far beyond the emotion of _____.

TWO WAYS TO FEAR GOD
1. Awesome _____

2. Astonished _____

God's greatness and majesty reduce us to an overpowering sense of awe that is not focused only on His wrath and judgment but on His transcendent _____.

WHY WE SHOULD FEAR GOD
1. Because of who He _____
   The very _____ of God—His unequaled majesty, His unparalleled magnificence, His unmeasured beauty—should cause us to fear Him.

2. Because of what He has _____
   Perhaps the most spectacular demonstration of God's work in the past is _____ itself.

3. Because of what He is _____
   Every breath we take is a precious gift of God's sustaining _____. And for that sustenance God deserves our fear—our never-ending _____.

PROMISES FOR THOSE WHO FEAR GOD
1. The promise of _____

2. The promise of _____

3. The promise of _____

4. The promise of _____

5. The promise of _____ _____

*USE THE FOLLOWING QUESTIONS TO DISCUSS
THE DVD SEGMENT WITH YOUR GROUP.*

What did you appreciate most in Dr. Jeremiah's teaching?

What does it look like in practical terms to fear God in your daily life?

When have you experienced awesome dread during an encounter with God?

When have you experienced astonished devotion?

Respond to Dr. Jeremiah's statement: "The very nature of God—His unequaled majesty, His unparalleled magnificence, His unmeasured beauty—should cause us to fear Him. There is no one like Him, and this is the primary focus in the Bible for the awe He should inspire in us."

How would you summarize what God has done and is doing in your life?

Review the five promises Dr. Jeremiah listed for those who fear God. How have you seen these promises come true?

APPLICATION. Be aware of situations this week that make you feel afraid—movies, TV shows, news reports, conflicts with others, dangerous or threatening circumstances, and so on. Seek to transform your fear in these situations.

THIS WEEK'S SCRIPTURE MEMORY. Use the memory card at the back of the book to memorize this verse:

> *The LORD takes pleasure in those who fear Him,
> In those who hope in His mercy.*
> PSALM 147:11

ASSIGNMENT. Read week 6 and complete the activities to conclude this study. Consider going deeper into this content by reading chapter 10 in Dr. Jeremiah's book *What Are You Afraid Of?* (Tyndale, 2013).

GOOD FEAR?

As we've explored various types of fear throughout this study, we've approached fear primarily as something negative. And there's a good reason for that.

We've seen, for example, that the fear of failure often prevents us from striving for the success God desires in our lives. We've seen that fear contributes to depression and disconnection. We've seen that fear increases the discomfort of disease and transforms death into a terrible threat rather than a welcome journey home.

There are times, however, when fear is an appropriate reaction to a given situation. If you come across a large bear in the woods, for example, reacting with fear is both natural and healthy. It may save your life! Or fear can be positive if it prevents you from taking physical or emotional risks that aren't in your best interest, such as jumping off a building or into an unhealthy relationship.

Here's another situation in which fear is both an appropriate and positive response: the fear of God.

I know that phrase is unpopular with many people these days, including people in the church. Some people believe the concept of fearing God is something to be avoided. It seems too negative. It makes God too unapproachable.

But I don't mind telling you that I disagree with such beliefs. In fact, I believe the fear of God is an essential element in the Christian life because of God's nature and His work. He's God! He's the Creator and Sustainer of the universe, and we who exist entirely for His purposes and entirely by His power would do well to remember those realities.

More importantly, we as Christians should embrace the fear of God because it's both a biblical concept and a biblical command. As we'll see this week, reacting with awe and reverent fear is the only proper response to our encounters with the living God.

DAY 1

APPROACH GOD WITH AWESOME DREAD

We're going to end our study by exploring the fear of God this week, and again I want to recognize that people can have different definitions of the word *fear*. Indeed, the idea of fearing something can run the gamut, all the way from minor annoyance to outright terror and dread. So exactly what do we mean when we talk about fearing God?

How would you summarize what it means to fear God?

I believe a scene from C. S. Lewis's Narnia book *The Silver Chair* illustrates one aspect of the fear of God. In the story a schoolgirl named Jill finds herself alone and desperately thirsty in an unknown wood. She knows nothing of Aslan, the Christ figure in these stories. But when she comes on a stream, she sees the great Lion between her and the water. Though her thirst is overpowering, Jill freezes in her tracks, too petrified either to advance or to run.

"If you're thirsty, you may drink," the Lion says.

Terrified and afraid she will be eaten, Jill doesn't move. She says, "Will you promise not to—do anything to me, if I do come?"

"I make no promise," the Lion answers.

"I daren't come and drink," Jill replies.

"Then you will die of thirst," the Lion tells her.

Jill says she will go find another stream, but the Lion responds with certainty, "There is no other stream."[1]

In what ways does this scene reflect God's character?

Maybe you're feeling a little confused right now. Maybe you're wondering, *Can the fear of the Lord really be compared to the feelings of a child quivering in unmitigated terror at an all-powerful being who forces hard choices and can do anything to anyone at any time?*

Actually, yes. Fearing God consists of two main components, and one of them is reacting to His incredible power with what I refer to as awesome dread.

MORE THAN A BUDDY

Many of us in the church have been programmed to view God primarily as a friend—as a divine buddy with whom we can hang out and shoot the breeze. This idea isn't entirely inaccurate, for Jesus Himself referred to us as His friends:

> *No longer do I call you servants, for a servant does not know what his master is doing; but I have called you friends, for all things that I heard from My Father I have made known to you.*
> JOHN 15:15

Because of this view of God, we've come to understand the fear of the Lord primarily in terms of awe and reverence. We've been told that to fear God means to stand in awe of Him, much as we would stand in awe at the majesty of the ocean or the beauty of a mountain range.

But we need to balance the equation. The truth is that God is much more than a friend, and the biblical concept of fear carries a much stronger meaning than simple reverence.

How have you experienced God as your friend?

When have you felt afraid of God or experienced fear in His presence?

When we look to the Scriptures, we begin to understand that fear is an essential element in our relationship with God. In fact, I would say a proper fear of God serves as the foundation for that relationship. We can't move forward as members of His kingdom until we gain a realistic understanding of His power in relation to our weakness. And when we gain that understanding, we'll naturally experience fear.

This kind of fear goes beyond awe and reverence when it's expressed in the Bible. Some people in the Bible certainly experienced awe in God's presence, but in most situations the biblical writers used words to convey fear when they wanted to communicate the idea of being genuinely afraid.

For example, here's the first time the idea of fearing God appears in the Scriptures:

> *The Lord God called to Adam and said to him, "Where are you?" So he said, "I heard Your voice in the garden, and I was afraid because I was naked; and I hid myself."*
> GENESIS 3:9-10

If you remember the context of this passage, Adam and Eve had just committed the first sin by eating the forbidden fruit together. And I assure you that what Adam felt in that moment was much more than awe and reverence for his Creator. He was stone-cold afraid. And that's exactly what he should have felt, because God had warned him that if he ate of the forbidden fruit, he'd die (see v. 3).

What's the connection between sin and the fear of God?

As human beings, we don't fear what we don't know. That's why little ones touch hot stoves once—and only once. In the same way, people who are without God are without fear of Him, so they don't hesitate to act in immoral ways. In Romans 3 Paul made a long list of complaints about ungodly people, and in verse 18 he concluded by quoting Psalm 36:1: "There is no fear of God before [their] eyes."

In contrast, those who know God fear Him. In fact, they find this fear so overwhelming that they can't even stand on their feet in His presence.

Read the following passages of Scripture and record what they contribute to your understanding of what it means to fear God.

Exodus 3:1-6

Matthew 17:1-8

Acts 9:1-9

FEARING JESUS

Many Christians today seem to think the incarnation eliminated the need for any fear of God. In Jesus, God came to earth in the form of a man, giving us an accessible God—one we could love and relate to as a friend. Those who adopt this mindset as the *entire* truth often describe Jesus as a gentle, compassionate, loving person.

Jesus was and is all that, but there's more. Once again, we need to remember the full picture, including incidents like this:

> *He found in the temple those who sold oxen and sheep and doves, and the money changers doing business. When He had made a whip of cords, He drove them all out of the temple, with the sheep and the oxen, and poured out the changers' money and overturned the tables. And He said to those who sold doves, "Take these things away! Do not make My Father's house a house of merchandise!"*
> JOHN 2:14-16

What's your initial reaction to this passage? Why?

The Book of Revelation also contains some terrifying depictions of our Lord. Remember John's reaction on seeing Christ in all His glory for the first time? He fell at Jesus' feet as though he were dead (see Rev. 1:17)! This wasn't a voluntary act of worship but an instinctive reaction of fear.

It wasn't a surprising reaction either. Even though John had known Jesus personally and had even laid his head on Jesus' chest (see John 13:25), he had no way to prepare for a glimpse of Christ in His full glory. John was completely overwhelmed by the majesty of the glorified Son of Man.

On an emotional level, do you feel different about Jesus than you do about God the Father? Explain.

The apostle Peter showed us what's perhaps the primary reason for our fear and dread of God. When Jesus guided Peter to a miraculous catch of fish after an unsuccessful night of fishing, Peter reacted in a way we might find surprising:

> *When Simon Peter saw it, he fell down at Jesus' knees, saying, "Depart from me, for I am a sinful man, O Lord!"*
> LUKE 5:8

In short, fear and dread are natural responses of the imperfect to the perfect, of the marred to the beautiful, of the contaminated to the pure, and of the powerless to the powerful. Fear is the foundation of our relationship with God because we can't help being afraid when we're confronted by His holiness.

I believe we've lost our sense of how far our sin separates us from God. As a result of sin, Paul tells us in Romans 5, we were actually God's enemies. As imperfect, marred, contaminated, powerless sinners, we can't imagine what it will be like to stand—or try to stand—in the august presence of the most beautiful, perfect, pure, and powerful Being in the universe.

Do you experience an appropriate amount of genuine fear in your relationship with God? Explain.

What obstacles prevent you from more regularly encountering and responding to God's holiness?

Tomorrow we'll explore the second aspect of what it means to fear God. But I'll conclude today with a passage from the prophet Isaiah. Let these words inform your attitudes and actions this week as you seek to serve our holy God:

> *The Lord of hosts, Him you shall hallow;*
> *Let Him be your fear,*
> *And let Him be your dread.*
> ISAIAH 8:13

DAY 2

APPROACH GOD WITH ASTONISHED DEVOTION

Do you remember the last time you felt astonished? I don't mean mildly interested in something or even surprised by something unexpected. I'm talking about the last time your jaw dropped to the floor—the last time something threatened to knock your socks off and leave you speechless.

When was the last time you felt astonished?

Paul Thigpen wrote about being astonished when he stood behind Niagara Falls for the first time. He could hardly cope with the colossal scale of the natural wonder—the powerful display of unleashed energy, the ear-splitting tumult of the waters plummeting and crashing onto the rocks below.

Why did Thigpen feel such fear? He was well protected from any possibility of falling in. Rationally, he knew he was perfectly safe. Yet his heart pounded. It was impossible for him to avoid thinking of what could happen if his body were hurled downward by that surging flood. He'd be crushed, obliterated. His imagination pushed everything from his mind except the awesome fear those falls evoked.

As we think about fearing God, we'd do well to remember that Niagara wouldn't make God's top-10 list of spectacular creations. Not even close. Those tons of plummeting water are less than a drop in the bucket compared to the galaxies He's tossed throughout the heavens.

For that reason Thigpen asks:

> How much more should our hearts pound with fear in His presence? We're only grains of sand on the shore of His infinity, fleeting seconds in His eternity. He is utterly greater than all the greatness we've ever witnessed, fantastically more powerful than all the powers we've ever encountered, inconceivably more intelligent than all the most brilliant minds we've ever known or known about.[2]

Yesterday I claimed that there are two aspects connected with fearing God. The first aspect is awesome dread, which I believe to be the starting point of our relationship with Him. Whenever we truly encounter God as a Being far above us in every way, we naturally feel afraid. We can't help being afraid.

The second aspect of fearing God is what I refer to as astonished devotion. Once we've established a proper foundation for our relationship with God—once we've seen the immense chasm between His holiness and our sinfulness—we begin to balance our fear and dread with something new.

As we'll see over the next few pages, the more we grow as disciples of Jesus and children of God, the more we're able to express our fear of the Lord through astonished devotion.

TO FEAR AND FOLLOW

In the Book of Romans the apostle Paul confidently expressed this truth for those of us who follow Jesus:

> *There is therefore now no condemnation to those who are in Christ Jesus, who do not walk according to the flesh, but according to the Spirit. For the law of the Spirit of life in Christ Jesus has made me free from the law of sin and death.*
>
> ROMANS 8:1-2

Having experienced salvation, children of God can now live with absolutely no fear of God's wrath. Our sins have been forgiven, and the penalty has already been paid through the death and resurrection of Jesus. That's an assurance engraved in eternity.

To what degree are you still afraid of God's wrath and judgment?

1   2   3   4   5   6   7   8   9   10

Not afraid   Terrified

How does freedom from God's wrath affect your life as a disciple of Christ?

These truths bring up an interesting set of questions. If Christ has removed the need for fear of God's wrath, do we really need to fear God at all? In other words, why should we continue to fear God if His grace has already taken away the consequences of His wrath?

These questions point to the two aspects of fearing God. It's true that active followers of Jesus no longer need to be terrified of God's wrath, so we experience less of the first aspect—awesome dread. Instead, we express our fear of God more and more through astonished devotion.

What, then, is astonished devotion? It's the aspect of fearing God that has the most application for active Christians. We fear God by honoring, reverencing, and cherishing Him. His greatness and majesty reduce us to an overpowering sense of awe that's focused not only on His wrath and judgment but also on His transcendent glory, which is like nothing else we can confront in this world. It leaves us all but speechless.

How would you summarize the concept of astonished devotion in your own words?

When has an encounter or experience with God led you to astonished devotion?

Does this mean Christians no longer experience awesome dread as part of fearing the Lord? Not necessarily. That aspect of fear is still the healthy basis of all other fears we have for God, such as awe and respect. After all, God's omnipotence, His consuming holiness, and His right to judge make Him worthy to be feared. But when you add to these character traits those that are warmer and more appealing by human standards—His love, compassion, grace, mercy, and patience—we stand in astonishment at the revelation of His character.

Though God had every right to judge the human race, in astounding mercy He sent His own Son to take that judgment for us. So to fear only God's power with trembling and dread without fearing (or respecting) His astonishing love is an incomplete response that diminishes our experience and enjoyment of Him. We need both awesome dread and astonished devotion.

How would you describe the relationship between awesome dread and astonished devotion in the Christian life?

As he so often does, A. W. Tozer has just the right words to describe this combined experience of fearing the Lord:

> I believe that the reverential fear of God mixed with love and fascination and astonishment and admiration and devotion is the most enjoyable state and the most purifying emotion the human soul can know.[3]

BIG FEAR AND LITTLE FEAR

One significant result of this balanced approach to fearing God is that it gives us perspective on the other fears we've discussed throughout this study. That's because the nature of fear is subjective. It changes from moment to moment and from experience to experience, based on what we're afraid of.

The threat of serious illness is a perfect example. We can spend our days worrying about a host of daily challenges and circumstances that aren't very important in the long run. But if the word *cancer* is mentioned in the same sentence with our name, all our daily anxieties disappear into the cloud of a bigger fear.

In other words, big fears make little fears go away.

What are some of the big fears in your life right now?

How have those fears influenced your decisions and priorities?

In the same way, when we truly fear God, our fear of other things and other people begins to wane. There's a natural progression. When other fears take precedence over the fear of God in our lives, we get into trouble.

That's what happened to the Israelites who lived during the time of Isaiah. Read God's words for the people of Judah:

Of whom have you been afraid, or feared,
That you have lied
And not remembered Me,
Nor taken it to your heart?
Is it not because I have held My peace from of old
That you do not fear Me?
ISAIAH 57:11

In losing its fear of God, the nation of Judah had become unduly afraid of false pagan gods. It no longer felt astonished devotion because it had lost the wonder of who God is.

Where have you seen evidence that believers today have lost the fear of God?

What obstacles or temptations prevent you from experiencing the fear of God more fully?

How will you seek to overcome those obstacles and temptations in the days to come?

To fear God is to understand who He is and to experience awesome dread at His holiness compared with your sinfulness. To fear God is also remembering what God has done to secure forgiveness for your sins and responding to Him with astonished devotion. May both of these aspects of fear lead you to a more meaningful experience of God's greatness and power this week and beyond.

DAY 3

WHY WE SHOULD FEAR GOD

As a pastor, I've heard more than my fair share of questions that begin with *why*. In addition, I've observed that even when people know the right thing to do, they still want to know why they should do it. They still want to understand and agree with the underlying principles that make it right.

I understand the motivation behind these questions. No one enjoys being told to simply follow orders—not on a long-term basis anyway. Nor is that a solid foundation for any relationship characterized by love and respect.

So as long as we remember that God is ultimately in charge and acknowledge that we don't always understand His ways, I believe it's appropriate to explore the *why* question in connection with the commands and encouragements in Scripture.

> **What emotions do you feel when you're forced to take an action without understanding why that action is necessary or important?**

> **How important is it for you to understand the why behind the actions you take?**
>
> 1   2   3   4   5   6   7   8   9   10
>
> Not important   Very important

Let's spend time today exploring why it's important for us to fear God as followers of Christ. We've already seen that the Bible commands us to fear God and that obeying those commands will lead us to experience awesome dread and astonished devotion in our relationship with Him.

Furthermore, the Scriptures also help us understand three primary reasons it's vital for us to fear God: because of who He is, because of what He's done, and because of what He continues to do today.

WE FEAR GOD BECAUSE OF WHO HE IS

The very nature of God—His unequaled majesty, His unparalleled magnificence, His unmeasured beauty—should cause us to fear Him. There's no one like Him, and this is the primary reason He should inspire awe in us.

I like the way Psalm 89 addresses this idea through the use of questions:

> *Who in the heavens can be compared to the LORD?*
> *Who among the sons of the mighty can be likened*
> * to the LORD?*
> *God is greatly to be feared in the assembly of the saints,*
> *And to be held in reverence by all those around Him.*
>
> **PSALM 89:6-7**

The implied answer, of course, is no one. God is in a class by Himself throughout the universe, which is one of the most compelling reasons we should fear Him.

What kinds of experiences or encounters with God remind you of His elevated place in the universe?

The prophet Jeremiah sounded like a lawyer addressing a jury when he made a similar case about the necessity of fearing God because of who He is:

> *Inasmuch as there is none like You, O LORD*
> *(You are great, and Your name is great in might),*
> *Who would not fear You, O King of the nations?*
> *For this is Your rightful due.*
> *For among all the wise men of the nations,*
> *And in all their kingdoms,*
> *There is none like You.*
>
> **JEREMIAH 10:6-7**

When it comes to wisdom, power, and other worthy attributes, there's no one like our God.

WE FEAR GOD BECAUSE OF WHAT HE'S DONE

When we begin to recognize God's supreme place in the universe, we fear Him simply because of who He is. Sometimes this fear causes us to run from God. When we're aware of our own smallness and shortcomings, the reality of an omnipotent and omniscient Creator may cause us to flee for a time.

When have you felt like running away from God?

In most circumstances, however, catching a glimpse of God's unparalleled character causes us to draw closer to Him. The recognition of God's supremacy motivates us to learn more about Him. And when we begin learning about God and His work in this world, we inevitably begin to fear Him because of what He's done.

That's what God's people experienced in the Old Testament. For example, look at the Israelites' reaction to being freed from slavery in Egypt and miraculously escaping through the Red Sea:

> *The Lord saved Israel that day out of the hand of the Egyptians, and Israel saw the Egyptians dead on the seashore. Thus Israel saw the great work which the Lord had done in Egypt; so the people feared the Lord, and believed the Lord and His servant Moses.*
>
> EXODUS 14:30-31

How would you explain the connection between fearing God and believing in Him?

I believe modern Christians sometimes feel jealous of the Israelites and other historical people mentioned in the Bible. We wonder what it must have been like to witness God do so many amazing things firsthand. We think, *If I'd seen what they saw and experienced what they experienced, I'd be at a much higher level of spiritual growth.*

We need to be careful about such thoughts, however, because they discount the amazing blessing we've been given in the complete canon of God's Word.

Don't disregard your complete access to the Scriptures. What a privilege to read the Bible and witness all the wondrous things God has done throughout the story of redemption—from Adam and Eve to Jesus to the church and beyond.

How have you recently been blessed by your access to God's Word?

In what ways do your encounters with the Bible lead you to fear God?

Another way we can encounter God's work in the past is by looking to creation. For example, the psalmist reminds us that the created world gives us additional cause to fear the Lord for what He's done:

> By the word of the LORD the heavens were made,
> And all the host of them by the breath of His mouth.
> He gathers the waters of the sea together as a heap;
> He lays up the deep in storehouses.
> Let all the earth fear the LORD;
> Let all the inhabitants of the world stand in awe of Him.
> For He spoke, and it was done;
> He commanded, and it stood fast.
> PSALM 33:6-9

How have your encounters with creation inspired you to fear God?

WE FEAR GOD BECAUSE OF WHAT HE'S DOING

The fear of the Lord is a natural response whenever we're confronted with who God is and what He's done in the past. But what about the present? What's God doing in the world today and in our lives as individuals that drives us toward awesome dread and astonished devotion in His presence?

There are many answers to that question. God is never idle, and His efforts always bring about the fruit He desires. God is a God of justice (see Isa. 30:18) who punishes the wicked (see Isa. 13:11). At the same time, He's the source of every good thing we experience in our lives (see Jas. 1:17).

But let's focus on a specific work of God that's vital to all believers: forgiveness.

If you wonder why forgiveness should move us to fear, consider what God is doing for us, compared to what He could have done or what He did to His own Son on the cross. I think this psalm expresses it best:

> If You, Lord, should mark iniquities,
> O Lord, who could stand?
> But there is forgiveness with You,
> That You may be feared.
> PSALM 130:3-4

Forgiveness is a work that God is doing in our lives right now, putting our sins away from us and remaking us into His image. Think about how many times you've prayed for and received forgiveness for your sins. But how much awesome dread and astonished devotion does forgiveness generate in your heart? Has the incredible reality of Christ's work ever moved you to tears, or do you take His forgiveness for granted and move on with your life?

What's your response to the previous questions?

What ongoing works of God move you to fear and worship Him?

What steps can you take to more deeply appreciate the amazing things God has done and is doing in your life?

Our God is like no other, and we fear Him because of who He is. We fear God because of the wondrous things He has done. And we fear God because of the miraculous and gracious works He continues to do even today.

DAY 4

FEAR PROFILE: THE ISRAELITES

Many people in the Bible are described as being afraid in the presence of God. Adam was afraid of God after eating the forbidden fruit and becoming aware of his nakedness (see Gen. 3:10). David was afraid after God's wrath broke out against Uzza, who'd touched the ark of the covenant (see 1 Chron. 13:1-12). And the disciples were terrified when they saw Jesus walking on top of the water during a violent storm (see John 6:16-21).

But I think the following is one of the most frightening passages in all Scripture:

> *It came to pass on the third day, in the morning, that there were thunderings and lightnings, and a thick cloud on the mountain; and the sound of the trumpet was very loud, so that all the people who were in the camp trembled.* ***And Moses brought the people out of the camp to meet with God***, *and they stood at the foot of the mountain.*
> EXODUS 19:16-17, EMPHASIS ADDED

Imagine the scene when Moses told the Israelites they'd meet with God. Imagine coming out of your flimsy tent and preparing to stand in the presence of the Creator of the universe—the same Being who created you and who knows everything about you. Wouldn't you be terrified to meet your Maker?

What would be most frightening or uncomfortable for you about standing in God's presence?

How would you prepare yourself to encounter God in that way?

As we'll see, this was just the beginning of the Israelites' awesome dread and astonished devotion in the presence of their God.

FIRE AND SMOKE

If you've ever witnessed the force of nature in a powerful way, such as an earthquake or a hurricane, you can understand a bit of what the Israelites experienced when they stood at the base of Mount Sinai that day and met with God. The text continues:

> *Mount Sinai was completely in smoke, because the* Lord *descended upon it in fire. Its smoke ascended like the smoke of a furnace, and the whole mountain quaked greatly. And when the blast of the trumpet sounded long and became louder and louder, Moses spoke, and God answered him by voice. Then the* Lord *came down upon Mount Sinai, on the top of the mountain. And the* Lord *called Moses to the top of the mountain, and Moses went up.*
>
> **EXODUS 19:18-20**

This was the kind of day and the sort of experience you never forget.

What's your initial reaction to the previous verses? Why?

How do the previous verses use different senses and sensations to communicate the idea of awesome dread?

I want to emphasize again that what the Israelites experienced during this encounter with God went way beyond awe and reverence. I'm sure they felt awe and reverence to a large degree, but that wasn't all. They were also terrified. They were scared out of their wits—which was appropriate.

That leads to a potentially perplexing question: Is it possible to love God and fear Him at the same time?

How would you answer the previous question?

On many occasions throughout my 40 years of ministry, people have questioned me about the subject of God's judgment. Often they say something like this: "My God would never send anybody to hell or punish someone for doing evil. My God is a God of love." I usually answer by telling them their God doesn't exist. There's a God to love and there's a God to fear, and He's one and the same!

Didn't God judge His own Son as a demonstration of His love for the world? And didn't He then show His love for the Son He judged by raising Him from the dead? How silly to think that if He's a loving God, He can't also be a fearsome God. The two attributes complement each other.

This mingling of love and fear captures our response to two attributes of God: mercy and judgment. Paul addressed both in this passage from Romans:

> Consider the goodness and severity of God: on those who fell, severity; but toward you, goodness, if you continue in His goodness. Otherwise you also will be cut off.
> ROMANS 11:22

Does this verse seem encouraging or discouraging to you? Explain.

Let's get back to the Israelites. What were the consequences of their frightening and enlightening encounter with God?

> All the people witnessed the thunderings, the lightning flashes, the sound of the trumpet, and the mountain smoking; and when the people saw it, they trembled and stood afar off. Then they said to Moses, "You speak with us, and we will hear; but let not God speak with us, lest we die." And Moses said to the people, "Do not fear; for God has come to test you, and that His fear may be before you, so that you may not sin."
> EXODUS 20:18-20

Moses' explanation is important. God showed the Israelites His power to focus their attention on the need to obey Him and the law He was about to give them. The fear of God should point us to obedience as well.

FEAR AND PROMISES

When we consider both dimensions of the fear of God—awesome dread and astonished devotion—we discover that the Bible promises abundant benefits for those who hold these fears. In other words, the fear of God leads to a wide variety of blessings.

The following list of five promises summarizes why it's wise to fear God. I present them without much comment because I believe they'll minister to your heart in their raw beauty and blessing. First is the promise of provision:

> *Oh, fear the LORD, you His saints!*
> *There is no want to those who fear Him.*
> *The young lions lack and suffer hunger;*
> *But those who seek the LORD shall not lack*
> * any good thing.*
>
> **PSALM 34:9-10**

Next is the promise of protection:

> *Behold, the eye of the LORD is on those who fear Him,*
> *On those who hope in His mercy,*
> *To deliver their soul from death,*
> *And to keep them alive in famine.*
>
> **PSALM 33:18-19**

One of my favorites is the promise of purity:

> *As far as the east is from the west,*
> *So far has He removed our transgressions from us.*
> *As a father pities his children,*
> *So the LORD pities those who fear Him.*
>
> **PSALM 103:12-13**

Next is the promise of prolonged days:

> *The fear of the LORD prolongs days,*
> *But the years of the wicked will be shortened.*
>
> **PROVERBS 10:27**

Finally we have the promise of privilege. The prophet Malachi said God keeps the words of those who fear the Lord in a special book of remembrance:

> *Those who feared the L*ORD *spoke to one another,*
> *And the L*ORD *listened and heard them;*
> *So a book of remembrance was written before Him*
> *For those who fear the L*ORD
> *And who meditate on His name.*
> MALACHI 3:16

These are only a sampling of the outpouring of promises the Bible gives to those who fear the Lord.

What emotions do you experience when you read these promises?

Which of the previous promises do you appreciate most? Why?

How do these promises affect the choices you make each day?

These verses certainly undermine any notion that God is simply a power-hungry tyrant, riding roughshod over the human race to satisfy His galaxy-sized divine ego. On the contrary, when we fear God, we not only honor Him, but we also receive benefits. The awesome dread we experience in His presence leads to astonished devotion in our hearts and onward to eternal life in heaven with Him. That's the final blessing for those who choose to fear the Lord.

DAY 5

HOW TO FEAR GOD

In this study we've covered a number of common yet potentially debilitating fears: the fear of failure, the fear of depression, the fear of being alone, the fear of being sick, and the fear of dying. I imagine no one had to teach you how to be afraid of those realities.

For the most part, our fears come to us naturally, almost instinctively. Even when we aren't born with a specific fear, we can automatically develop it through life experiences. If we touch a hot stove, for example, the pain we experience teaches us to be afraid of fire. In the same way, when we suffer through a debilitating illness, it doesn't take much effort to develop a fear of disease. The connection happens subconsciously.

What fears have naturally or instinctively come into your life?

Which fears have you learned over time?

Things are different when it comes to the fear of God, however, because the fear of the Lord doesn't come naturally for most of us. It's something we learn and develop over time, based on our encounters with who God is, what He's done, and what He continues to do. Fortunately, we don't have to wait for this process to run its course. That's because the Bible makes it clear that the fear of God can be both taught and learned.

For example, look at God's instructions for Moses as He gathered the Israelites in advance of declaring the law:

> *Gather the people to Me, and I will let them hear My words, that they may learn to fear Me all the days they live on the earth, and that they may teach their children.*
> DEUTERONOMY 4:10

King David also believed the fear of God was something that could be and should be taught. He wrote:

> *Come, you children, listen to me;*
> *I will teach you the fear of the L*ORD.
>
> **PSALM 34:11**

> *Teach me Your way, O L*ORD;
> *I will walk in Your truth;*
> *Unite my heart to fear Your name.*
>
> **PSALM 86:11**

In the spirit of these words, let's conclude our study together by exploring what it takes to learn how to fear God.

FEAR AND GOD'S WORD

None of us who follow Christ today are kings—not in America at least. But we can learn a great deal about how to fear God from the way kings were trained in the culture of ancient Israel:

> *It shall be, when he sits on the throne of his kingdom, that he shall write for himself a copy of this law in a book, from the one before the priests, the Levites. And it shall be with him, and he shall read it all the days of his life, that he may learn to fear the* L ORD *his God and be careful to observe all the words of this law and these statutes.*
>
> **DEUTERONOMY 17:18-19**

What's your initial reaction to these verses? Why?

Every king who took the throne of Israel was required to learn the fear of the Lord by writing down God's law, keeping it in a priestly book, and holding it by his side for life. He was instructed to maintain a humble heart and be true to the commandments. If he did these things, he was promised that his days and the days of his people would be lengthened (see v. 20).

So how do we learn to fear God? Like the hopeful kings of old, we begin by reading and obeying the Word of God.

How would you describe your current experiences with reading and obeying God's Word?

In what ways has the Bible influenced your fear of God?

It wasn't just leaders who were expected to learn the fear of the Lord. God commanded all the people to gather every seven years for a special public reading of the law:

Gather the people together, men and women and little ones, and the stranger who is within your gates, that they may hear and that they may learn to fear the LORD your God and carefully observe all the words of this law, and that their children, who have not known it, may hear and learn to fear the LORD your God as long as you live in the land which you cross the Jordan to possess.
DEUTERONOMY 31:12-13

The message is clear: if you want to fear God, begin by consuming His Word.

Action step 1: Commit to a deeper experience with God's Word this week. Read the Book of James over the next five days—one chapter a day—and record any principles or commands you can obey as a way to express your fear of God.

FEAR AND REMEMBERING

Memorials were another great generational teaching tool the Israelites used to inspire the fear of God. For example, when the people of Israel crossed the Jordan River and entered Canaan for the first time, the Lord rolled back the waters of the river, creating a dry riverbed over which the Israelites could cross. This miraculous event recalled God's rescue of His people at the Red Sea.

To commemorate that event, God told Joshua to appoint 12 men, one from each tribe, to select a stone and carry it on his shoulders to Gilgal on the west side of the river. There Joshua set up the stones as a monument. He announced that in future times when children asked their fathers about the stones, the great story of God's faithfulness could be told. Why go to all that trouble to remember something?

> *[So] that all the peoples of the earth may know the hand of the Lord, that it is mighty, that you may fear the Lord your God forever.*
> JOSHUA 4:24

The principle is simple. When we intentionally seek to remember who God is and what He's done for us and especially when we teach these principles to the next generation, the fear of God increases. We learn to fear God by choosing to remember Him and His mighty acts.

> **Read the following passages of Scripture and record what they teach about choosing to remember who God is and what He's done.**
>
> Deuteronomy 6:4-9
>
> Numbers 15:37-41

I wonder if we're losing the fear of God in our churches and in our culture because we have no memorial stories to share with our children and grandchildren. Do we tell them how God has blessed us as we've lived a God-fearing life? Do we have any miracles that we can communicate to the next generation?

> **What are your answers to the previous questions?**

> Action step 2: Make a memorial this week to commemorate the primary ways God has blessed you. Be sure to communicate to your family the meaning of your memorial.

THE CONCLUSION OF THE MATTER

Solomon spent his life searching for meaning and significance in human existence. In the end he concluded that everything boiled down to the fear of God and its connection to obeying God in all things:

Let us hear the conclusion of the whole matter:
Fear God and keep His commandments,
For this is man's all.

ECCLESIASTES 12:13

The last words someone speaks before his death are often considered highly significant. Consider this statement from the last words of King David:

The God of Israel said,
The Rock of Israel spoke to me:
"He who rules over men must be just,
Ruling in the fear of God."

2 SAMUEL 23:3

Also consider the last words of Joshua, a mighty man of God:

Fear the LORD, serve Him in sincerity and in truth, and put away the gods which your fathers served on the other side of the River and in Egypt. Serve the LORD!

JOSHUA 24:14

What obstacles are currently preventing you from fearing God and serving Him more fully?

How will you begin to overcome these obstacles this week?

I'm thankful my God is a fearsome God. My love for Him is deeper because of the fear that complements His love. Though the storm rages all around, I'm safe and secure. I love my God. And I fear Him. And I love Him because I fear Him.

1. C. S. Lewis, *The Silver Chair* (New York: HarperCollins Publishers, 1981), 20–21.
2. Paul Thigpen, "Loving God, Fearing God: How Can We Do Both at the Same Time?" *Discipleship Journal* [online], July/August 2000 [cited 26 September 2013]. Available from the Internet: *navpress.com*.
3. A. W. Tozer, *Whatever Happened to Worship?* (Camp Hill, PA: Christian Publications, 1985), 30–31.

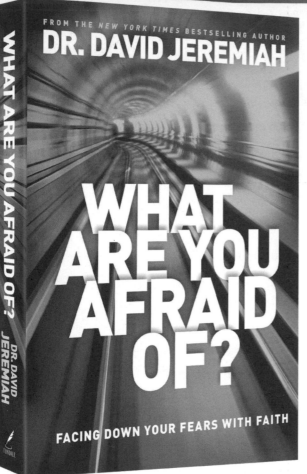